The Boys of
Shakespeare's School
in the
Second World War

The Boys of Shakespeare's School in the Second World War

Richard Pearson

Pen & Sword
MILITARY

First published in Great Britain in 2013 by
PEN & SWORD MILITARY
an imprint of
Pen and Sword Books Ltd
47 Church Street
Barnsley
South Yorkshire S70 2AS

ISBN 978 178159 152 9

A CIP record for this book is available from the British Library.

Printed and bound in England
by CPI Group (UK) Ltd, Croydon, CR0 4YY

Typeset in Times New Roman by
CHIC GRAPHICS

Pen & Sword Books Ltd incorporates the imprints of
Pen & Sword Aviation, Pen & Sword Family History, Pen & Sword Maritime,
Pen & Sword Military, Pen & Sword Discovery, Wharncliffe Local History,
Wharncliffe True Crime, Wharncliffe Transport, Pen & Sword Select,
Pen & Sword Military Classics, Leo Cooper, Remember When,
The Praetorian Press, Seaforth Publishing and Frontline Publishing

For a complete list of Pen and Sword titles please contact
Pen and Sword Books Limited
47 Church Street, Barnsley, South Yorkshire, S70 2AS, England
E-mail: enquiries@pen-and-sword.co.uk
Website: www.pen-and-sword.co.uk

King Edward VI School Stratford-upon-Avon

King Edward VI School (KES) can trace its origins to the thirteenth century, when in May 1295 a rector scholarum was appointed by the Guild of the Holy Cross to teach the basics of learning to the boys of Stratford. In the early fifteenth century, the guild established its headquarters in the timber-framed Guildhall and built Pedagogue House, which remains the oldest example of a purpose-built schoolhouse in England. In 1482, Thomas Jolyffe, chaplain of the guild, endowed the school with the income from lands in Stratford. Following the dissolution of the guild during the Reformation, King Edward VI granted a Royal Charter in 1553 that assured the future of the school, to be renamed The King's School. The upper floor of the Guildhall has been a schoolroom for 600 years, and is known throughout the world as the place where William Shakespeare was taught Latin, Greek and Rhetoric. Through centuries of political, religious and social upheaval, the school has continued to grow and flourish.

At the outbreak of war in September 1939, King Edward VI School remained a small grammar school, with 158 boys on the register. The headmaster had arrived before the First World War and most of the masters in the early 1920s. They represented stability, a continuance of contact with the boys and an establishment of a sense of permanence, and the school ethos was of service to the community and to the country.

Like the generation before them, the boys of King Edward VI School went to war in 1939 with similar determination and an absolute belief in the cause for which they were fighting. Through the Battle of Britain and the bombing campaigns, in Atlantic convoys and the Western Desert, the Mediterranean campaign, in Burma and the seas around Malaya, and in a German concentration camp, the fifty-two boys fought and died with fortitude and bravery. This book is dedicated to them.

Richard Pearson
Archivist
King Edward VI School
Stratford-upon-Avon
2013

Contents

List of Abbreviations

ASC	Aircrews Selection Centre
ASDIC	Anti-Submarine Detection Investigate Committee
ATC	Air Training Corps
BAF	Balkan Air Force
BEF	British Expeditionary Force
CCF	Combined Cadet Force
CRE	Commander Royal Engineers
EFTS	Elementary Flying Training School
ITW	Initial Training Wing
KES	King Edward VI School
LCP	Landing Craft Personnel
LCT	Landing Craft Tank
LZ	Landing Zone
MBE	Member of the Order of the British Empire
NCO	Non-Commissioned Officer
NFU	National Farmers' Union
OTC	Officer Training Corps
OTU	Operational Training Unit
RAF	Royal Air Force
RAFVR	Royal Air Force Voluntary Reserve
RAPC	Royal Army Pay Corps
RDF	Radio Direction Finding
RNZAF	Royal New Zealand Air Force
SEACTC	Southeast Air Corps Training Centre
SOE	Special Operations Executive
STS	Secret Training Schools
USAAC	United States Army Air Corps

Introduction
The Generation

The lads that will die in their glory
And never be old.
A.E. Housman, *A Shropshire Lad*

When the men returned from the Western Front in 1919, they believed that 'a land fit for heroes' – the promise made by Prime Minister David Lloyd George – would in some way compensate for the years of struggle and sacrifice made by the generation the poet Katherine Tynan Hinkson called 'the gay and golden boys', who had flocked to the colours. Joyful crowds filled the streets, bands played and flags were hung from the windows. There were celebrations and medals, and in Stratford-upon-Avon a memorial to those boys from the town who had fallen was eventually placed at the top of Bridge Street. The euphoria did not last. The promise was not kept. It was a bitter peace, and they returned, in the words of A.E. Housman, to 'the land of lost content'.

Following the cessation of hostilities, the years that followed saw a steady rise in the number of boys at King Edward VI School. These boys were the same as the previous generation who had gone to fight on the Western Front in that they threw themselves enthusiastically into the clubs, sports and societies that flourished in the school. But whereas the earlier boys had been inspired by the heroes in the books of Anthony Hope, Ryder Haggard and John Buchan, those boys, typical of that time, who grew up between the world wars, escaped with their imagination into the writings of Frank Richards and Captain W.H. Johns, enjoyed the adventures of Richmal Crompton's William, and seized the regular thrills and fun provided by the *The Gem, The Magnet* and *The Dandy*. Those who were not boarding travelled to school increasingly on bicycles, whilst one boy came on a motorcycle and, in time, one became the first to drive himself to school in an Austin motor car. Their backgrounds remained the same as they had been at the school for a hundred years, with their families working in the professions or in farming. The boarders lived in School House and those day boys not from Stratford travelled by bus or train from rural Warwickshire. There was no real rivalry between the two groups, except during the annual rugby match, when feelings ran very high. And it was primarily the boarders who formed the backbone of the many societies, whilst the Stratford day boys were able to attend those late afternoon or evening meetings.

There was a potent enthusiasm in the life of the school, and this was in large part due to the leadership of the headmaster, the Reverend Cecil Knight, who had arrived on the eve of the outbreak of the war in 1914. Alive to innovation, he also treasured the traditions and antiquity of the school. Possessing great humanity and a delightful sense of humour, he was also very strong on discipline and demanded constant effort. He endeared himself to this generation of boys, and the loss of so many of them in another war was a grievous blow.

In 1914, the school magazine *The Stratfordian* reported that: 'In view of the emergency, Mr Knight at once instituted a cadet corps, and many of the first NCOs were soon on the fields of Flanders.' From the early days of borrowed uniforms and dummy rifles, the Combined Cadet Force (CCF) formed a company in the 3rd Cadet School Battalion of the Royal Warwickshire Regiment and in due time acquired a drum and bugle band. Following the guidelines established by the War Office 'to provide a disciplined organization in a school so that pupils may develop powers of leadership by means of training to promote the qualities of responsibility, self-reliance, resourcefulness, endurance and perseverance', the cadets drilled each week in the school quadrangle, where there was a rifle range, and they went on annual camps and visits to the battlefields in France and Belgium.

This was a generation that grew up in an environment of social uncertainty and fragile economy. The lost cause of patriotism that had been enthusiastically and fatally embraced by their fathers' generation was replaced by disillusionment and then a determination to build a secure future.

Life in Stratford-upon-Avon resumed, with its cattle and produce markets, the annual regatta on the Avon, dances in the Hippodrome and the Corn Exchange, and the summer festival at the Shakespeare Memorial Theatre. There were picnics on the banks of the river in fields of primroses, and country walks across the Welcombe Hills and along the lanes of Loxley through meadowsweet and celandines, and in woods of bluebells and dog's mercury. Stratford Rugby Club played its first season since 1914, and the Old Edwardians XV reformed successfully. From a bicycle bought from Sleath's in High Street, boys cycled through the Warwickshire lanes past fields of ox-eye daisies and woodbine. Their school uniform came from Fred Winter in High Street, their hair was cut at Rumsey's in Henley Street, and the treat of tea and cake could be enjoyed at the Hathaway Tea Rooms in High Street or the Corona Café in Wood Street.

The effects of both national and international developments swept through Stratford in these inter-war years. Hunger marchers trudged through the streets on their way to petition Parliament, and the British Union of Fascists held a boisterous meeting in the Hippodrome on Wood Street. Somewhat muted during the years of the Great War, the Shakespeare Birthday celebrations were enthusiastically resumed and by the early years of the 1920s had become international, with the German swastika flag memorably flown in Bridge Street in 1939 – surely a harbinger of coming events in Europe. The secretary of the Stratford branch of the League of Nations Union voiced his gloomy prediction in 1937 that war clouds were gathering, and the mayor appealed for volunteers to help in filling sandbags to place around public buildings and in the construction of air raid shelters. Having built their own in the school grounds, boys from King Edward VI School happily volunteered to help build shelters in Rother Street. The *Stratford-upon-Avon Herald* advised 'the need for being prepared' whilst conceding that the possibility of an air raid on Stratford was 'remote'. Some thirty-five senior boys from the School volunteered as messengers for the Air Raid Precaution organization, attending courses at the headquarters in Henley Street, where they were told about the colour, smell and persistency of different gases and were fitted with the 'civilian duty' gas masks.

Articles and poems in *The Stratfordian* reflected the growing awareness appreciated by the boys in the relentless approach to another war. This generation dreamt of flight, read the weekly air papers and were forever looking upwards. As soon as they could, boys joined the Royal Air Force Volunteer Reserve (RAFVR) or one of the local flying schools. They embraced the traditional British values of bravery, honesty and fair play, and the adventures of Biggles brought the energy and daring of youth. Owen Dudley Edwards wrote that these young pilots learned their ethics from Frank Richards' stories about Greyfriars School in *The Gem* and *The Magnet*, which both enjoyed an enormous circulation. Harry Wharton and his chums distrusted authority and knew that they had to stick up for one another and stand up to bullies. The stories captured a world that contrasted with the birth of an age that knew all about its rights but had forgotten its responsibilities.

In the Great War many joined up from a sense of patriotic duty, and were then disillusioned. Their motivation after that point was sometimes no more than a will to survive. This feeling was less common amongst those who took part in the Second World War. They were not driven by the memory of the human devastation of the trenches of the First World War, nor the traumas of the survivors. Instead, most felt they were fighting for a proper moral cause that had been expressed by Neville Chamberlain on 3 September 1939 in his radio address on the outbreak of war: 'It is evil things that we shall be fighting against, brute force, bad faith, injustice, oppression and persecution.'

These boys of King Edward VI School represent a generation that believed war would bring Western civilization to an end and that the only fate worse than this would be to live in a fascist state. They felt themselves, wrote Sebastian Faulks in *The Fatal Englishman*, to be a generation without ancestry, because the Great War had killed 10 million and cut them off from the past. 'A new war, they believed, would eliminate also the possibility of a future.' The fighter pilot Richard

Hillary came to share this belief, although with the important qualification that victory by the Allied forces against Germany would stamp forever on the future of civilization those values of honesty and fair play for which all the boys of his generation had died.

Slowly, sadly, inexorably, these boys and their generation are fading from our memories. So many stories, too many to tell, but these of the Old Boys of Shakespeare's school will help to keep memories alive, and their adventures are our legacy.

Chapter 1

STANDISH CECIL MOTTRAM
Flying Officer, Pilot, 101 Squadron
7 March 1940

With expanded wings he steers his flight
Aloft, incumbent on the dusky air.
John Milton, *Paradise Lost*

E ngland in January 1940 was plunged into extraordinarily cold weather, with the south of the country recording the coldest temperatures for more than a hundred years. Icy storms from the North Sea swept over East Anglia, and the flat, rich fields were blanketed with heavy snow. The dark, long-tailed Dartford warblers perished and did not reappear in the gorse and hedgerows for fifty years, when milder winters returned. Transport was paralysed, and the bitter winds swept across the fens and the airfields at Bircham Newton, Marham and Mousehold Heath.

Leaflets over Germany.

The Blenheim.

Five miles from Fakenham, near where the river Wensum flows, Royal Air Force (RAF) West Raynham was the base for 101 Squadron, which in the early months of 1940 flew Bristol Blenheim bombers on scores of weather, maritime reconnaissance and mining sorties, and inundated Western Germany with propaganda leaflets. At the outbreak of the war, President Roosevelt appealed to the belligerents to renounce the bombing of civilian targets, and the editorial in the *Daily Mail* of January 1940 hastened to concur: 'We are fighting for a moral issue. We should do nothing unworthy of our cause.' Air Marshal Arthur 'Bomber' Harris was to later comment caustically, 'My personal view is that the only thing achieved was largely to supply the continent's requirements of toilet paper for the five long years of war.'

The leaflet operation served the useful needs of reconnaissance and training. Enemy territory was observed, including identifying the effectiveness of blackout, the activity of airfields, the position and accuracy of searchlights and anti-aircraft guns, and movements by road, rail and water. So, night after night, the bombers plodded monotonously across the North Sea with their bundles of leaflets, plus the occasional empty beer bottle fitted with a razor blade in the neck, so that it whistled like a bomb as it fell towards the ground.

The Bristol Blenheim was designed and built as the direct result of a public challenge to the aircraft industry from Lord Rothermere, in 1934, for a high-speed aircraft to regain the title of fastest civilian aircraft, and to challenge the fast aeroplanes being developed in Germany. Ordered directly from the drawing board and first flown in 1935, it carried a crew of three – pilot, navigator/bombardier, and wireless operator/air gunner.

A number of modifications led to the Blenheim Mk IV, which, by 1939 and the outbreak of war, had a fixed rearward-firing Browning machine gun in the port engine nacelle, designed solely as a 'frightener', a rear-firing gun under the cockpit, and a single Browning machine gun in the turret. It was issued to every Command – Bomber, Coastal and Fighter. Regarded as a pleasant aircraft to fly, it possessed, wrote Julian Humphries in his history of the Bristol Blenheim, a number of characteristics that could catch even experienced pilots by surprise. Moreover, with the rapid advances that had been made in technology since all its modifications, by the time the Blenheims went to 101 Squadron at West Raynham, they were already obsolescent and their flaws were brutally exposed by enemy fighters. In action it was quite incapable of surviving an efficient attack and could stand little punishment. It was not an aircraft to give confidence to the inexperienced. Under attack, a Blenheim's only chance of survival was to find cloud or to attempt a hedge-level escape.

Following an inconsequential attack on Wilhelmshaven on 4 September by ten Blenheims, any action during the rest of the autumn of 1939 was predominately limited by the weather, the lack of information and the limited nature of the German fleet movements.

Standish Mottram joined 101 Squadron at West Raynham in January 1940. He had enlisted directly from university in 1938, and *The London Gazette* of 15 November 1938 announced that he had been granted a permanent commission as a pilot officer with effect from 29 October 1938. Becoming a flying officer in 1939, he was sent to RAF Wyton, between Huntingdon and St Ives, where he trained battle pilots on Blenheims.

From his home in Newbury in Berkshire, where he had attended Marlborough House Prep School in Reading, Standish arrived as a boarder in School House at King Edward VI School in 1930. Within his first year he had established a reputation for enthusiasm and reliability, and became a dependable member of both the Photographic Society (led by the redoubtable physicist Denis Dyson) and the Shakespeare Society (where he took part in productions in the fifteenth-century Big School, where William Shakespeare received his education). This generation of boys at King Edward VI participated actively in the life of the school with a competitive spirit, and this was particularly reflected in the many sporting activities and teams that flourished.

Becoming Captain of School House – the attractive, tall, early nineteenth-century building on Chapel Lane (that was also the home of the headmaster) –

Standish Mottram in School House.

KES Cadet Corps, Mottram top left.

Mottram won his 1st XV colours. Tall and strong, *The Stratfordian* reported that he was 'a sound captain who sets a good example', and 'had creditably undertaken the unenviable position of "hooking"'. He joined the KES Boat Club in 1932, and was a member of the 1st IV, which won the meritorious Ball Cup in 1935, and in the same season he won the Brickwood Skulls (presented in 1928 by Sir John and Lady Brickwood as a prize for rowing). An effective sergeant in the school's Cadet Corps, he took his part in a number of Shakespeare's Birthday parades and camps. In the summer of 1935, Standish secured a place at St Catherine's College, Cambridge, to read Engineering. In his final year, he stroked the 'Rugger Boat' and gained his oar, and graduated with his BA in Engineering Studies.

At Wyton, Flying Officer Mottram trained pilots in the Blenheim Mk I, which continued in service with home-based bomber squadrons in spite of it having been superseded in the bombing roll by the Blenheim Mk IV. The usefulness of the Mk I remained because it was able to serve as a conversion trainer and as a crew trainer in Operational Training Units (OTUs). With his move to West Raynham, the training continued in the Mk Is, but also in the Mk IVs.

Standish's experiences in the RAF were very similar to many of his generation who had enlisted from university or straight from a sixth form in a grammar or public school: usually some flying in the morning, then, after lunch, some squash or tennis, and time to clean up before tea. They spurned the vulgarity of a bar. Drinks were brought to the ante-room by a waiter summoned by a bell, and signed for by chits. Their world was so attractive and they created a unique culture for themselves. They soared over the Downs, the Chiltern Hills and the Weald. 'We were young,' one of them remembered. 'You could do anything when you were young.'

Airfields sprung up close to sedate little villages and quiet market towns in East Anglia, where tradition had remained undisturbed for generations.

Life during those early months of 1940, as the winter made way to a milder spring, was made more tolerable by visits to the Samson and Hercules ballroom in Norwich and The Star public house in nearby Fakenham. It was still the time of the 'Phoney War', that period that marked a lack of any major military operation, but training and operations continued and, on Thursday, 7 March, Flying Officer Mottram took off in Blenheim Mk IV NG165 on a training flight over Wainfleet Sands on the Lincolnshire coast. It was part of a programme of air firing, local altitude and photography, and the Blenheim was making a wireless transmitter range test on reduced power.

Flying low, south-west of Diss, near the village of Botesdale in Suffolk, at 2.45 pm the Blenheim struck a line of high tension cables, took down two telegraph poles and a high chimney, and crashed into the garden behind the White Horse public house in Rickinghall Superior. The wireless operator, Corporal Hartland, sustained injury and survived; both Standish Mottram and his navigator, Sergeant

WHITE HORSE
PUBLIC HOUSE

THE BLENHEIM PILOTED BY STANDISH CECIL MOTTRAM...

...TOOK OFF THIS CHIMNEY POT

← TOOK DOWN THIS
TELEGRAPH POLE

← TOOK DOWN THIS
CHIMNEY ENTIRE

RICKINGHALL STREET c. 1930

The White Horse Hotel, Rickinghall Superior.

Mottram's grave in Highgate Cemetery.

Alfred Mawdsley, were killed instantly. Almost immediately, the crash site was surrounded by members of the local Home Guard. Local boys hurried to the spot in an attempt to find souvenirs, but the Home Guard had been supplemented by RAF ancillary staff. What remained of the plane was cleared within a few days. Sergeant Mawdsley was buried in Wallasey (Rake Lane) Cemetery in Cheshire.

Standish Mottram, the first of the King Edward VI Old Boys to be killed since the outbreak of war, was twenty-three years old. His grave in Highgate Cemetery in London is a rustic design topped by a tall cross in a corner of the cemetery that is rather overgrown with oxalis and yellow-flowered pontentilla. He is commemorated in the Memorial Library at King Edward VI School and on the KES Boat Club Memorial in the Garden of Remembrance in Stratford-upon-Avon.

Had we but world enough, and time
Andrew Marvell, *To His Coy Mistress*

Chapter 2

ALAN HENRY WOODWARD
Flight Sergeant, Observer, 144 Squadron
20 March 1940

Brief had their lives been until then, nor much longer endured
Edward Shanks, *The Few*

C aptain W.E. Johns, himself a First World War pilot, wrote the first book featuring the pilot and adventurer James Bigglesworth, nicknamed Biggles, in the story *The White Fokker*, which appeared in the very first issue of *Popular Flying* magazine in 1932. In the same year, a collection of Biggles stories was published, priced two shillings and sixpence, as *The Camels are Coming*. Biggles mixed his own adventures with those on behalf of the British Secret Service. He represented a particular type of hero, like John Buchan's Richard Hannay, that combined professionalism with a gentlemanly air, and personified the sort of hero that appealed to boys: a calm, confident and competent leader. These stories captured the imagination of boys who were also avid readers of *Popular Flying* (also edited by Captain W.E. Johns), published monthly, priced sixpence, and *Flying*, published each Friday and priced threepence.

Biggles – The Black Peril.

Flying promised to open the world that had captivated the mind of the young Alan Woodward as he had listened to his geography master, Tom Barnsley, firing his imagination with talk of vast continents, great rivers and exotic people. Flying meant travelling to far-flung places with unlimited horizons. This was such a contrast to the quiet rural life in South Warwickshire that gave Alan such enjoyment, where old farmers wore smocks and their wives churned butter in the age-old way; there was the coppice covered with wild strawberries and ragged robin; the horse pulled the plough along the old furrows; there were hot biscuits and homemade blackberry jam; and mechanization on the farm was still in the future. Sheep grazed on the hillsides, cattle roamed the pasture land, and wheat and barley ripened in the sun. In the countryside that Alan knew, life remained as it had been for a hundred years.

Alan Woodward attended King Edward VI School between 1931 and 1938, and his contemporaries included many who were to live to mourn the loss of friends and then to die themselves. He grew to excel in sports, whether it was fives, cricket or rugby. *The Stratfordian* reports his development in these where the competition was fierce and the standards were high. He gained his colours in a 1st XV that was particularly determined, and he was a dependable middle-order batsman in a successful 1st XI. Becoming a prefect in 1937, he was also made Captain of Flower House (named after Charles Edward Flower, the driving force behind the restoration of the school buildings in 1892), and became a member of the Dramatic Society, playing Drawcansir in a production of *The Rehearsal*, in which his friends Richard Spender played Bayes, the author, and Geoffrey Cross played the Second Stage Keeper.

The only son of William and Mabel Woodward of Stratford, Alan left KES in April 1938 when he was in the Sixth Form, and anxious to realize his ambition to fly, he joined the Worcestershire Flying Club based at Pershore. Gaining his pilot's 'A' licence, he entered the RAF Navigation School in North Shropshire, 6 miles from Shrewsbury, flying both single- and twin-engined airplanes, and from there was posted to 144 Squadron at RAF Hemswell. Situated between Lincoln and Scunthorpe, Hemswell was a bomber base that flew the Hadley Page Hampden

Worcestershire Flying School.

9

Mk I. With a crew of four in rather cramped conditions, the Hampden was a fast, twin-engined medium bomber with better manoeuvrability than its counterpart, the Blenheim.

At home on leave when war was declared, Alan returned to his squadron and, during the late months of 1939, took part in a number of flights over enemy territory, including the Heligoland Bight and dropping propaganda leaflets (called 'nickels') over Hamburg and other towns. 61 Squadron was also based at Hemswell and, flying Hampdens, they were the first of Bomber Command to drop bombs on Germany on the evening of 19 March, the target being the Hörnum seaplane base on the northern German coast used by the Kriegsmarine.

The following night, Wednesday, 20 March, Alan and two other crew members left Hemswell in a Hampden Mk I (L4137) on a training flight over the Lincolnshire coast. Returning to the

Alan Woodward.

airfield, the pilot lost control and the Hampden plunged into a steep dive and crashed near Scunthorpe. All the crew members were killed. Alan was nineteen. It was the week before Easter and the gardens in Stratford-upon-Avon were alive with lilies, daffodils and narcissi.

On Easter Monday, St Andrew's Church in Shottery was decorated with daffodils, hyacinths, cinerarias, palms and arum lilies, and following a service conducted by the Reverend W.H. Harrison and his old headmaster, the Reverend Cecil Knight, Alan was buried with full military honours in the Warwickshire earth that he had loved so well. As three Hampden bombers soared overhead and dipped in salute, the coffin, draped in the Union flag, was carried into Stratford Cemetery by three friends and members of the KES Cadet Corps – Sergeant Major Richard Spender, Staff Sergeant Kingsley 'Budge' Francis and Quartermaster Sergeant Roland Brisley, plus Signaller Walter Dyson from Alan's squadron and members of the Royal Air Force. Three additional members of the RAF were in attendance. Amongst the many wreaths laid on the grave from his friends and family were ones from the staff and boys at King Edward VI School, the President and members of the KES Old Boys' Association, the Old Edwardians RFC, plus the rugby and tennis clubs. Flowers were also laid from the Mayor of Stratford-upon-Avon, RAF Hemswell and the Commanding Officer of No. 5 Group RAF, who spoke of Alan's 'quiet and unruffled temperament'.

Alan Woodward is commemorated on the memorial at RAF Hemswell, the memorials in Holy Trinity Church and the Garden of Remembrance in Stratford-upon-Avon, and in the Memorial Library at King Edward VI School.

When duty whispers low – thou must
The youth replies – I can.
Ralph Waldo Emerson, *Voluntaries*
Engraved on Alan Woodward's headstone in Stratford-upon-Avon cemetery

Stratford-upon-Avon Cemetery.

11

Chapter 3

PHILIP ANDREW TYLER

Leading Aircraftman, Air Gunner, 37 Squadron
1 May 1940

I open the casement into his room
So tidy and neat
And the sun shines in and chases the gloom
And the wind blows sweet
Ready for him early or late
I hear the click of the garden gate
But it is not he.
May Hill, *The Click of the Garden Gate*, 1940

The decision by Germany to invade Norway on 9 April 1940, and worked out using an old Baedeker guide, was made for both strategic and economic reasons. The port of Narvik, which remained ice-free in winter, was the western terminal of an isolated railway line that connected the Swedish iron ore mines at Kiruna, from where Germany obtained 10 million tons of iron ore. In order to secure this supply, and also to obtain bases from which to attack Britain's trans-Atlantic supply lines, an attack on both Norway and Denmark (which was geographically in the way) was planned during the winter of 1939-1940. The Royal Navy pursuit of the German supply ship *Altmark* into Norwegian waters in February 1940 determined the Germans to attack as a preventive manoeuvre against a planned French and British occupation of both these countries, during which Britain had made a desperate flurry of anti-shipping strikes to impede the German invasion of Norway. Winston Churchill, as First Lord of the Admiralty, urged the laying of a minefield inside Norwegian territorial waters in order to cut the vital iron ore link.

The invasion of Denmark on 9 April lasted less than six hours. The campaign in Norway lasted longer and was not completed until 10 June. Simultaneous landings were made at Oslo, Kristiansand, Trondheim and Narvik, and at Bergen and Stavanger, the main ports of Western Norway.

Philip Tyler attended King Edward VI School between 1930 and 1936, and

Landings at Stavanger.

during his senior years was a member of the Debating Society (one motion he tabled questioned the value of 'prep'), on the committee of the Photographic Society, played for the 2nd XV, and was made a prefect and sergeant in the Cadet Corps. In 1935 he went to Belgium with the cadets to Mons – marching along the actual route taken by the retreating British forces in 1914 – also visiting Marche-les-Dames, Namur and the Brussels Exhibition. The school numbered just under 200 boys and it was a time of keen competition, discipline and encouragement. Entrance was by interview by the headmaster, there were fees for boys not living in Stratford, boarders were still in School House, and the Prep School in The Old Vicarage took boys from the age of six until they moved on to KES.

Philip Tyler.

Leaving school at Easter 1936, Philip crossed Church Street to work in the offices of the National Farmers' Union Mutual Insurance, but it was not for him. Although, like so many boys of his generation, he was anxious to join the Royal Air Force, to his great disappointment he failed the medical examination. Undeterred, he underwent corrective surgery, first in the Stratford Hospital and then the Birmingham General Hospital, and this enabled him to pass the test and join the RAF on 8 June 1937 at the Training Wing at Uxbridge. Posted to the technical training college at RAF Henlow in Bedfordshire to train as a wireless operator, he completed the course in September 1938 and was posted to 37 Squadron. He joined RAF Feltwell, south of the village and 10 miles from Thetford on the edge of the Fens, where he trained as an air gunner and was allocated as air crew on 28 February 1939. Completing a course at RAF Sealand in Flintshire, he was promoted to Leading Aircraftsman on 3 September and completed his air gunner course on 24 November. He was at RAF Feltwell when war was declared on Sunday, 3 September 1939. Within seven hours, the squadron went into action in the Wellington Mk I, with a sweep over Heligoland Bight to attack German warships, but failed to locate them because of bad weather conditions and failing light.

With a maximum speed of 234 miles per hour and a ceiling of 18,000 feet, the Wellington (along with the Blenheim) was the workhorse of Bomber Command during the first months of the war. Its weaponry comprised two .303 machine guns in the nose, two .303 machine guns in both the turret and the tail turret, plus a bomb load of 4,500lbs. It had a wingspan of 86 feet 2 inches, and a length of 64 feet 7 inches.

The next big raid on the German coast was on 18 December and included Wellingtons from 37 Squadron, 149 Squadron (from RAF Mildenhall) and 9 Squadron (from RAF Honington). It was so disastrous that Wellingtons were subsequently barred from flying near the shores of Germany in daylight. Caught in a cloudless sky, they were pounced on by Messerschmitt Bf 109 and 110 fighters, guided for the first time by German radar. Philip's squadron lost five of its six aircraft. As a result of this, Wellingtons were fitted with armour plate and self-sealing fuel tanks.

Into the spring of 1940, 37 Squadron continued night sorties over Germany, with raids over Kiel, Sylt and Berlin – a round trip of 1,180 miles – to drop thousands of propaganda leaflets. In April, with the war moving to Scandinavia, actions were concentrated on Norwegian targets. During this time, following a raid and on the way home, Philip, as the wireless operator, would filter music like the popular *Indian Summer* from his radio down the intercom.

At 5.35 pm on Tuesday, 30 April 1940, Wellington Mk I P9213, piloted by Squadron Leader Ridley Bradford, took off from Feltwell for operations over Stavanger, Fornebu and Aalborg airfields. Fifty aircraft were dispatched: twenty-four Whitleys, sixteen Wellingtons and sixteen Hampdens. The bombers flew over the airfield at Stavanger in successive waves of attack, destroying buildings and aircraft, but came under attack from batteries of anti-aircraft guns that circled the field and searchlights lit up the sky. A huge explosion led one pilot to later report: 'The German's must have had a Brock's fireworks benefit night. The Air was alive with blue and orange searchlights, rockets and shells, which burst into groups of stars.'

As the bombers turned for home, the German fighters pounced, making beam attacks, to which the Wellington's had no reply owing to their limited fields of fire. Wellington Mk I P9213 with Philip Tyler and the five other members of its crew was last seen in combat with an enemy flight off the Norwegian coast. It was one of two Wellingtons and one Whitley lost on the raid; a further four aircraft crashed in England. All in all, Bomber Command lost thirty-one aircraft on raids to Stavanger for so little result.

It is now known that Philip's Wellington was shot down south-west of Stavanger by Oberfeldwebel Erwin Sawallisch, flying a Me 109. Sawallisch had been a member of the flying section of the Kondor Legion, which fought in the Spanish Civil War. He became one of the German air aces of the Second World War, with thirty-three 'kills', subsequently flying on the Eastern Front and in North Africa. He was shot down on 19 August 1942, and his body was found on the beach of the Mediterranean.

This was not known to Philip's family and his mother never quite accepted his loss. The *Stratford-upon-Avon Herald* of 3 May 1940 reported that his parents had been notified that Philip was missing. Both they and his fiancée, whom he planned to marry in June, remained hopeful and believed that he was still alive – even after all the British forces withdrew from Norway on 8 June and the receipt of an official notification saying, 'Although formal action to presume death for official purposes will not be taken until a further period has elapsed, it is feared that all hope of finding him alive must be abandoned.' Believing that he was a prisoner of war, his mother kept his room ready and his bed made.

Philip is commemorated in the RAF Book of Remembrance at St Clement Danes Church in the Strand in London, on the plaques in the Garden of Remembrance in Old Town, Stratford-upon-Avon, and in the Memorial Library at King Edward VI School, originally built in memory of those thirty-one Old Boys of the school who died in the First World War. He is also remembered on the Royal Air Forces Memorial at Runnymede overlooking the Thames and the meadow where the Magna Carta was sealed by King John in 1215. The land was donated by Sir Eugen and Lady Effie Millington-Drake, and the memorial, designed by Sir Edward Maufe, commemorates more than 20,000 aircrew lost without trace. Consisting of a shrine embraced by a cloister in which the names of the missing are recorded, the memorial was opened on 17 October 1953 by Queen Elizabeth II, who declared that 'wherever and for as long as freedom flourishes on the earth, the men and women who possess it will thank them and will say they did not die in vain.'

There's purple lilac in your little room
And somewhere out beyond the evening gloom
Small boys are culling summer watercress.
Of these familiar things I have no dread
Being so very sure you are not dead.
Anna Gordon Keown, *Reported Missing*

Chapter 4

LEONARD JOHN MERRITT
Sergeant, Observer, 107 Squadron
12 May 1940

If I take the wings of the morning
And remain in the uttermost parts of the sea,
Even there also shall Thy hand lead me;
And Thy right hand shall hold me.
Psalm 139

His father travelled extensively on business and Leonard Merritt spent the first years of his senior education at Prince Henry's Grammar School in Evesham. He arrived at King Edward VI School in early May 1928, and remained until the end of December the same year. Charged by the exploits of Albert Ball VC, the air ace who had been killed during the First World War, Leonard was successful in joining the Royal Air Force Halton Aircraft Apprentice Scheme, which had been established in 1920 by Lord Trenchard 'to provide the services with a cadre of highly motivated airmen who would play a vital part in a future conflict'. He strongly believed that mastery of the air had to be gained and retained through offensive action. Serving as the commander of the Royal Flying Corps in France from 1915 to 1917, Trenchard was appointed Chief of the Air Staff in 1918 and discovered that there was a very short supply of specialist ground crew.

Originally located at RAF Cranwell, the Apprentice Scheme was moved permanently to RAF Halton, near Aylesbury in Buckinghamshire. Entrance to the Apprentice Scheme involved a highly competitive examination, intelligence and aptitude tests, and a medical examination. Admittance was exclusively limited to boys between the ages of fifteen and seventeen-and-a-half, and the RAF assumed legal guardianship of the boys as in *loco parentis*. It was a three-year course over five days a week and included both practical and academic training, plus basic military training. Proud to be known as 'Trenchard's Brats', a considerable number of the apprentices went on to achieve air rank.

Successfully passing out of the Apprenticeship Scheme, Leonard entered an air force that was experiencing an uncertain future. In the bitter struggle to retain the very existence of the RAF as an independent service, Trenchard argued that aircraft provided an opportunity to wage an entirely new kind of war. The Army and the Royal Navy greeted his prophecies with memoranda in which conventional courtesies failed to mask a withering scorn. But throughout the 1920s he gathered around himself in the middle ranks of the RAF a body of passionate disciples who were inspired by his vision of air power. The Royal Air Force stood at the centre of public and political debate in the period between the wars, and military thinkers Basil Liddell Hart, Colonel J.C. Fuller and J.M. Spaight all argued the significance of aerial warfare and bombardment.

The old area organization of the Air Defence of Great Britain was replaced by Commands – Bomber, Coastal, Fighter and Training. Bomber Command's squadrons moved to eastern airfields that were closer to Germany and Leonard Merritt joined No. 2 Group and 107 Squadron at Wattisham, 2 miles north-east of the small Suffolk town of Bildeston.

Within a day of the declaration of war, 107 Squadron, with the other resident squadron at Wattisham, the 110, were in action with a raid on German warships near Wilhelmshaven – the same raid undertaken by Philip Tyler's 37 Squadron. The pocket battleship *Admiral Scheer* was attacked at low level, being hit four times. At high level against the *Scharnhorst* and the *Gneisenau* in the Elbe, the squadron scored no hits. Only one of Squadron 107's aircraft returned from this operation, still with its bomb load intact.

The concept of the self-defending bomber formation, fighting its way over enemy lines to attack vital targets miles behind any battlefield, lay at the core of the theory of strategic air power. The power-operated gun turret represented a major British breakthrough in armament technology, and it was believed that it gave the RAF bombers a decisive margin of protection against an attacking fighter. Bomber Command reported that the German fighters had failed in response to the raid, and that it was enemy anti-aircraft fire that was responsible for all the RAF losses. Nevertheless, two bombers had been destroyed by Me 109 fighters and it was decided that future raids would be carried out at higher levels.

During the remainder of 1939 and into the spring of 1940, 107 Squadron, together with 110 Squadron, made many day and night raids against a variety of targets including seaplane bases and U-boats. However, these raids on enemy territory were costly for the Blenheim bombers, as it became all too evident that they were vulnerable to the Messerschmitt 109E fighter.

These were heady days for Leonard Merritt. The Blenheim squadrons were the bomber element of the Advanced Air Striking Force in France, and during the winter they continued to make regular although very costly attacks into Germany.

In April 1940, there were raids on the German-occupied European mainland. The weather always presented problems – it was either too clear and the bombers were picked off by fighters, or too cloudy so the target could not be found. So operations were changed to the night, leading to fewer losses, but the bombing proved to be less accurate.

On 10 May 1940, Winston Churchill became Prime Minister, the day Germany launched 'Case Yellow' and the Panzers smashed into Luxembourg, The Netherlands and Belgium. By 17 May, the Battle of France was a week old and there had been several anti-shipping attacks by 107 Squadron to impede the German invasion of Norway. In France it was decided that the RAF would support the Army by attacking German communications rather than their forward positions, and only 2 Group's Blenheims, tragically inadequate, were risked on daylight ground support operations.

The Dutch and Belgian coasts were kept under close observation, along with other areas where possible German seaborne raids or invading forces could be easily detected.

In the early morning of 12 May, a squadron of twelve Blenheims (wing strength), led by their charismatic commander Basil Embry, left RAF Wattisham in an attempt to halt the rapid German advance by attacking the bridges at Maastricht. Leaving at 8.10 am, the squadron joined up with twelve Blenheims from 15 Squadron, which had taken off twenty minutes earlier from RAF Wyton

The trio of graves for Keedwell, Berridge and Merritt, Voroux-Goreux Communal Cemetery at Fexhe-le-Haut-Clocher.

in Huntingdonshire. Each aircraft was heavily laden with four 250lb bombs in the bay and eight 40lb fragmentation bombs on external carriers. Attacking at 6,000 feet, it was a bloody confrontation as the squadrons were immediately engulfed in heavy anti-aircraft fire (flak) and numbers of rampant Me 109s. Hurricane fighters of 87 Squadron escorted the bombers and battled with the Me 109s, one flown by the ace Hauptmann Adolf Galland.

Coming under heavy fire, Blenheim Mk IV P4914, piloted by Pilot Officer Osborne Keedwell, with Air Gunner Aircraftsman Leslie Berridge and Observer Sergeant Leonard Merritt, crashed at 9.25 am near Voroux-Goreux, about 6 miles west of Liege. There were no survivors, and all three were buried in Voroux-Goreux Communal Cemetery at Fexhe-le-Haut-Clocher.

At the end of the day, the bridges remained intact and aerial photographs taken during the mission showed that all ninety-six bombs had missed their targets.

Leonard Merritt is remembered on the Old Haltonians Roll of Honour in St George's Church in Halton, near Aylesbury, and is commemorated in the Garden of Remembrance in Stratford-upon-Avon and in the Memorial Library at King Edward VI School.

As I leave this mortal frame, from human ties set free,
Receive my soul, O God of love, I humbly come to Thee.
Flight Lieutenant E.B. Impey, *The Airman's Prayer*

Chapter 5

HARRY ALFRED CHARLES SMITH

Lance Sergeant, 1/7th Battalion, Royal Warwickshire Regiment
27 May 1940

No gift have we now we may give them
That weighs what they gave.
Edward Shanks, *Triumphant Threnody*

Harry Smith arrived at King Edward VI School when he was eleven years old in 1926 and left at the end of his years in the Sixth Form in the summer of 1933. Born in Ashford in Kent, he came with his parents to live in Stratford-upon-Avon, first in Union Street then later halfway up the Banbury Road, a few houses from Richard Spender. Always known as 'Sonny', he was at school at a time of burgeoning sporting achievement: the formation of the school Boat Club and a succession of very successful crews; a strong series of 1st XVs and the establishment of a new pavilion on the playing fields at Manor Road; and a number of entertaining cricket XIs. Harry played regularly for the 2nd XV and gained his 2nd XI colours.

Like several of his friends and contemporaries, he began working in the offices of the National Farmers' Union Mutual Insurance on Church Street (now the headquarters of the Stratford-upon-Avon District Council). Formed in 1910 by seven local farmers with a working capital of £190, it provided insurance as an inducement for farmers to join the National Farmers' Union.

As the threat of a European war grew in the early spring of 1939, the Government announced on 29 March that the Territorial Army would be doubled in size. In Stratford-upon-Avon, Mayor Thomas Waldron appealed for men, and during what the poet Keith Douglas called 'the last summer of this hot time', Harry joined D Company, 1/7th Battalion, Royal Warwickshire Regiment, based at Elmhurst, near Holy Trinity Church.

In September 1939, the British Expeditionary Force (BEF), created by the British Government and authorized to be sent to France in the event of war, took up defensive positions along the French-Belgian border, with four regular infantry divisions and fifty light tanks. They were going to hang out their washing on the Siegfried Line, the line of defensive tank defences and bunkers that stretched for 390 miles from Kleve on the border with The Netherlands and along the western edge of Germany to Weil am Rhein on the border with Switzerland. By 14 May, one more regular and five more divisions from the Territorial Army had arrived. Now 394,165 men were in France, with 237,319 assigned to front-line service.

The German offensive that began on 10 May proceeded at a breathtaking pace. On the northern flank the Dutch surrendered within five days, and on 18 May the Belgian Army surrendered unconditionally. General Fedor von Bock and Army Group B attacked the BEF on 14 May, pushing the Allied Front back

Harry Smith.

towards the French frontier. General Gerd von Rundstedt and Army Group A invaded France through the Ardennes. Rundstedt's offensive cut communications between French and British Commands, and left the BEF surrounded on three sides. Within ten days of the launching of the offensive, the advance had covered 150 miles, and by the night of 20/21 May had reached the Channel coast. The Germans' 'sickle plan' had worked. The Allied forces had been cut in two, with vast numbers squeezed between the coast and the oncoming German divisions.

An attempt to halt the advance at Arras on 21 May could not be sustained and the British commander, Lord Gort, decided to withdraw to Dunkirk so that his forces could be evacuated to Britain. More than 300,000 were rescued from the beach using a range of crafts, from pleasure boats to Navy destroyers. A rearguard action was being fought by members of the BEF just east of Dunkirk on a defensive line that in reality was little more than a string of fortified farms. On the morning of 27 May, the order was given: 'Position to be held at all costs – there will be no further withdrawal.' During the heated exchange of fire, Sonny Smith was killed.

Hastings added: 'Few of the encircled troops had got away ... but the delay of forty-eight hours proved vital in enabling the British to orchestrate the extraordinary retreat – a masterpiece of improvisation accompanied by much good luck.'

Camarades!

Telle est la situation!
En tout cas, la guerre est finie pour vous!
 Vos chefs vont s'enfuir par avion.
A bas les armes!

British Soldiers!

Look at this map: it gives your true situation!
Your troops are entirely surrounded —
 stop fighting!
Put down your arms!

Propaganda leaflet.

At this time, Dunkirk was a military disaster, but victory was plucked from defeat, and so the myth began. Churchill wrote that there 'was a white glow, overpowering, sublime, which ran through our island from end to end.'

On Friday, 31 May, Harry Smith's parents received the news – as did Jean Stratford of Greenhill Street, whom he had planned to marry – that he had been killed in action. Harry was buried at Bas-Warneton (Neerwaasten) Communal Cemetery at Comines-Warneton, south-east of Ypres in Belgium. Harry is commemorated on the National Farmers' Union Mutual Memorial in Tiddington, which records the sixteen members of staff who gave their lives in the Second World War; on the memorial in Holy Trinity Church, in the Garden of Remembrance in Stratford-upon-Avon; and in the Memorial Library at King Edward VI School.

Though the world has slipped and gone,
Sounds my loud discordant cry
Like the steel birds' song on high.
Edith Sitwell, *Lullaby*, 1940

Chapter 6

JESSE GEORGE STANLEY

Sergeant, Navigator, 18 Squadron
4 July 1940

Keep the home fires burning,
While the props are turning,
Keep the beacon flashing bright
Till the boys come home.
Ivor Novello/Lena Gilbert Ford, 1914

Jesse Stanley arrived at King Edward VI School in the autumn of 1927. One of his friends was Philip Hillier, who became a flight lieutenant, was awarded the DFC, and was killed in action in Egypt in 1942. Jesse's family were farmers in Shipston-on-Stour, and when he finished his schooling in 1932, he returned to work on the farm. He remained there for several years before joining the Royal Air Force Volunteer Reserve, trained as a navigator, and when war was declared he was ordered to report to 18 Squadron.

Blenheim.

18 Squadron comprised No. 70 Wing at RAF Upper Heyford in Oxfordshire, flying Bristol Blenheims as part of the No. 2 Group. The Wing went to France as part of the British Expeditionary Force Air Component (aerial reconnaissance) flying from an airfield near Roye-Amy in Picardy. The unit was withdrawn to England in early summer after most of the squadron had been lost in those frenetic months in France. A note in April 1940 reads: 'Records lost during the evacuation from France.' So little is known of their activities prior to their arrival, and the records open in May 1940 showing that the squadron's aircraft arrived at RAF Watton on 26 May. The residents, 82 Squadron in their ordered ranks, were bewildered at morning parade when a handful of scarecrows fell in, dressed in fragments of uniforms, bandages and tin helmets. These were the survivors of 18 Squadron. Their commanding officer requested that his three remaining aircraft should be attached to 82 for operations that day. They flew with fighter escort to attack a reported panzer division laagered in a French wood. Instead they found a British Red Cross column. They returned home intact except for one Blenheim of 18 Squadron, whose unusual camouflage markings were mistaken by a nervous Hurricane pilot for those of a Junkers 88, and was shot down with no survivors.

From RAF Watton the squadron moved to West Raynham, south-west of Fakenham in Norfolk, on 12 June, where it was re-established to its proper number of fifteen Blenheim bombers.

On Thursday, 4 July, Jesse Stanley took off as part of a group from RAF West Raynham in Blenheim Mk IV L8866 for a 'gardening sortie' (minelaying) operation on North West Germany. On the flight home it was attacked west of Rotterdam by a Messerschmitt 109 flown by Unteroffizier Gunther Behse. The effect can be understood by a description of Me 109s closing fast on a Blenheim:

> The first bursts of fire began to clatter through the fuselage. It felt as if they were in a corrugated iron shed with someone bouncing dried peas on the roof. The windscreen shattered, then the propeller sheared from the port engine and spun glittering away towards the sea. The oil pressure on the starboard engine began to drop rapidly as oil poured from a fractured line.
>
> Patrick Bishop, *Bomber Boys*

At 12.10 pm, L8866 plunged into the Maas estuary west of Rotterdam.

The crash was witnessed by a local fisherman, Anton van der Zee: 'We had been fishing on the Brielseplaat and rowed towards Zwartewaal. It was low tide and we saw something floating on the north shore that we could not identify. After we had rowed closer, we found that it was a corpse, we thought a German likely to have been killed in Rotterdam. Since there was low tide we could not hang the corpse behind the boat and we therefore decided to warn the Germans that they could pick up their own comrade. When I arrived at City Hall I told the German on duty and he asked us to go with him to retrieve the body, and with another fisherman we dragged the body to the grass next to the pier. When he discovered that it was an Allied aviator, the German lost all interest. The body was that of the pilot, Flight Lieutenant Ivor Worthington-Wilmer, and he was buried in the cemetery at Zwartewaal.' On 6 July, while attempting to retrieve the crashed Blenheim, the body of Sergeant George Maydon was found and buried in the dunes of Oostvoorne with a cross made of rough wood, with the inscription: 'Maydon'. The body of Sergeant Jesse Stanley was never found.

On 25 July, George Maydon's remains were excavated by the people of Oostvoorne and buried with military honours in the local cemetery.

Memorial in Newbold-on-Stour.

Following the raid on 4 July, all the other Blenheims returned safely to West Raynham. Unteroffizier Gunter Behse subsequently went missing after combat with RAF fighters south-west of Southend in the Thames Estuary on 5 September 1940.

Jesse Stanley is commemorated on the Royal Air Forces Memorial at Runnymede, on the war memorial on the village green in Newbold-on-Stour, and in the Memorial Library at King Edward VI School.

No gravestone in yew-dark churchyard
Shall mark their resting place
Paul H. Scott, from a poem engraved on the
window of the Runnymede Memorial

Chapter 7

JOHN GARLAND MILLER
Pilot Officer, 149 Squadron
12 August 1940

If I had my way we would never grow old …
… but some never grew old.
Lou Klein

When John Miller, and hundreds like him, decided to join the Royal Air Force, they would be sent to an aircrew reception centre. The most well known was in St John's Wood in London. This was known as 'arsy tarsy', where the transformation from civilian to Leading Aircraftsman (LAC2) took place and where they were 'kitted out', given an introduction to service life and a little preliminary drill. Posted to an Initial Training Wing (ITW) they were given the basics of flying theory, parade ground drills and service protocols, and sorted into aircrew trades training, whether pilot, observers' school, wireless or gunnery school. Posted under training, they were then sent to an Elementary Flying Training School (EFTS), where, following fifteen hours' training, the pilot went solo or was sent to learn another trade. Following the EFTS, pilots were moved to an Advanced Flying Training School, where they would receive additional training for single- or multi-engine flying. The other aircrew trades passed from the ITW to an Elementary Training School in their speciality – wireless, gunnery, navigation or bomb aiming – and then they also went on to Advanced Training. Finally, they were all posted to an OTU and there was to be no more arbitrary assembling of men. It was clearly understood that the fate of Bomber Command hung on the integrity and mutual confidence of the operational crews, and so every possible step was taken to allow like-minded souls to fit together.

The 'crewing up' process at the OTU was a haphazard affair but in most cases highly successful. Hundreds fresh out of flight training were herded into hangars and told to sort themselves into crews. There was a given number of each crew trade, enough to produce a given number of crews. Usually a pilot started the process by picking a bomb aimer or a navigator and asking them if they would like to fly with him. Then they would look for the other members of the crew.

What attracted individuals to one another ranged from physical appearance to smoking or drinking habits, and the crews that resulted from this strange 'marriage' of individuals tended to be very diverse in background and nationality. It looked like anarchy but it worked. Thus formed, the crew would train at the OTU. The success of a bomber squadron ultimately depended on the quality of the individual crews and the serviceability of its equipment. Aircrew and ground crew needed to be a tight, cohesive team since they spent most of their time with their own crew. They were a self-contained unit, dependent on each man knowing that the others would do their jobs well and have confidence in their judgement and skill.

John Miller.

So, at the end of their training these rather bewildered but intensely willing young men went to their squadrons. John Miller had enlisted in August 1939 and was sent to the Operational Training Unit at Moreton-in-Marsh in Gloucestershire – where he passed out as a pilot – and from there, with his five crew members, was posted, the youngest member of 149 Squadron, to RAF Mildenhall to fly Wellington Mk I bombers over Germany. Cecil Beaton wrote of bomber crews that: 'The motive of their existence carries them to a skyline to which we cannot follow. They possess the secret ecstasy of the mystic.' They were the innocents who cultivated a rakish air and drank at The Angel in Bury St Edmunds and The Bell in Thetford.

That idyllic summer of 1940 the crews were driven out night after night, orders and bomb loads being changed at a moment's notice as crisis followed crisis. As the sense of a familiar flying club faded and the squadrons saw their pre-war personality vanish and die, the pain was acute.

John Miller was born in Somerset, where his family were farmers, and he attended Taunton Grammar School until the family moved to Alveston Pastures Farm on the Loxley Road, just outside Stratford-upon-Avon. He was fifteen years of age when he arrived at King Edward VI School and he immersed himself in a variety of activities, playing for both the 2nd XV and 2nd XI, as a member of the Cadet Corps, and in a memorable production of *The Two Gentlemen of Verona*, performed in the headmaster's garden beside the old Mulberry tree on Benefactors' Day in 1934. John appeared as The Host alongside his friends Cyril Thornton, who played an outlaw, and Thomas Testar, who appeared as Panthino. Farming and the outdoors were always dear to him and he became an enthusiastic member of the Natural History Society, giving a lecture on the subject of animals in the English countryside.

Leaving school at eighteen, John took over the family farm but also travelled over to Radford Semele, just beyond Leamington Spa, to the farm of the Thornleys, who were close family friends and who also owned the brewery there.

It is easy to imagine that a future of an outdoor life while introducing new ideas and developing mechanization would have been a happy one for John, but when war was imminent in August 1939 he decided, like his younger brother Rogers, to join the Royal Air Force. So in the late spring of 1940 he arrived at Mildenhall.

At home on leave at the beginning of August John became engaged to a young lady from Moseley, which at that time mostly comprised large houses built for Edwardian middle-class families. Returning to Mildenhall, he received a flying visit from his brother Rogers, a pilot officer in 609 Squadron, who had been given permission to fly his Spitfire from his base in Wiltshire. It was their final meeting.

On Monday, 12 August, a Wellington Mk I, piloted by Pilot Officer John Miller, took off from RAF Mildenhall at 9.35 pm for a raid on Gelsenkirchen in the North Rhine-Westphalia area of the Ruhr, a flight of six hours. Twenty-eight Wellingtons were sent that night to attack an airframe factory at Gotha and an aircraft park at Diepholz. It was also an area with coal mining and oil refining. Returning to Mildenhall at 3.48 am, and while making its approach to land wide of the flare path, John's aircraft collided with a radio mast and crashed at Beck Row, a small village in West Suffolk. All six members of the crew were killed. It was the only Wellington lost on the raid that night.

A private family service was held on 15 August in the chapel at the crematorium at Perry Barr in Birmingham. John is commemorated on the Alveston War Memorial, in the Garden of Remembrance in Old Town, and in the Memorial Library at King Edward VI School.

> *If you live on the brink of death yourself, it is as if*
> *those who have*
> *gone have merely caught an earlier train to the*
> *same destination, and*
> *whatever that destination is, you will be sharing it*
> *soon, since you*
> *will almost certainly be catching the next one.*
> Flight-Lieutenant Denis Hornsey

Notes

1. The year after John and his crew were killed, the film *Target for Tonight* was made at RAF Mildenhall. It told of a Wellington bomber from 149 Squadron attacking an oil refinery in Kiel. All the parts were played by members of the squadron. The film won an Honorary Award at the 1942 Academy Awards.

2. On 6 August 1941, Armstrong Whitley Z6740 from 77 Squadron, on a training flight to RAF Wellesbourne, crashed on fire a few fields from Alveston Pastures Farm with the loss of all five airmen on board.

Rogers and John Miller's grave in Radford Semele.

Chapter 8

ROGERS FREEMAN GARLAND MILLER

Pilot Officer, 609 Squadron
27 September 1940

How brilliantly you flew for such short years,
Roger, across the small horizon of my life,
Like laughter, borne on shining wings!
Richard Spender

Historian Richard Overy considered the Battle of Britain 'the centre-point of British historical memory of the Second World War', and for the young men who fought, the battle 'was expressed in the language of the school playing field. The sporting metaphors were uniquely English.' The pilots were like hunters, wrote Cecil Day Lewis, ranging across the ribbed and shifting sky, with a fighting heart and a kestrel's eye. These young men alone had the reflexes for duels at closing speeds of up to 600 miles per hour.

Patrick Bishop wrote in *Fighter Boys* that whatever their differences of background, all these boys were children of their time. Their enthusiasms were stoked by what they read in the illustrated papers, which, aimed at the youth market, sold in thousands and each week were seized and read avidly. The boys recognized at once the change that old-fashioned swashbuckling married to modern technology would carry.

To fly was wonderful fun, but a profound and premature seriousness overtook most aerial warriors in the face of the stress and horror that they experienced every day they were exposed to operations.

These boys who were to join the Royal Air Force turned out to be the least long-sighted of warriors. They joined because they passionately, single-mindedly, unashamedly wanted to fly. The adventures of those pilots in the 1930s – Lindberg, Hinckler and Mollison – had seized the imagination of their generation. Their stories, wrote Bishop, were of almost unimaginable courage and skill. They were young men of conscience. 'In mankind's long history,' wrote Alan Fenton in *The Call of Destiny*, 'never had the issues been so clean cut. They were to fight an evil regime that had to be destroyed, and to do that they were ready to sacrifice everything.' Their spirit was exalted by the Battle of Britain in a fashion that enabled them to transcend the logic of their continuing strategic weakness against superior numbers. A backbench Member of Parliament declared that 'they must be a superb body of men.'

Rogers Miller (he was always known as Roger) decided on a career in flying while at school, where he was the band sergeant in the Cadet Corps. After passing his school certificate, he joined the RAF at Cranwell on a six-year commission in June 1939. Completing his training on 5 April 1940, he took the train to Chalford, in the Frome Valley of the Cotswolds. A mile and a half away was 5 Officer Training Unit at Aston Down, where he was trained in Hurricanes. After converting to Spitfires, Roger was

Rogers Miller.

posted on 4 May to 609 Squadron at Drem in East Lothian. In early June he was posted to RAF Warmwell, near Middle Wallop in Dorset.

Middle Wallop, 5 miles west of Andover, became operational on 12 June 1940, and fell within No. 10 Group Fighter Command. With its headquarters at Rudloe Manor, near Box, Middle Wallop became an operational sector station with 'Y' Sector Operations Room. The squadrons chiefly based at Middle Wallop were 234 and 238 with Hurricanes, and 609 with Spitfires. All Middle Wallop squadrons used RAF Warmwell as an advanced base, flying down early in the morning and returning at dusk. During the Battle of Britain, when Roger was there, Warmwell had only very primitive facilities, and the 609 pilots' dispersal was a canvas tent – which very often blew down – pitched on the northern boundary beside the road from Higher Woodsford to West Stafford. The pilots would sit in deckchairs, smoking, reading a book or newspapers, listening to the wireless or playing chess.

The pilots of 609 were all rather suave. Some customized their blue uniforms with scarlet linings, always, of course, with the top button undone. They took to wearing blue ties because the RAF's standard black seemed to them too gloomy, and they also wore silk cravats, because the constant twisting left and right (known as 'the Messerschmitt twitch') as they searched for enemy aircraft chafed their necks. Roger wore the silk 1st IV colour rowing scarf that he had been awarded at school.

At King Edward VI School, he always had a particular affinity for rowing, and was a member of the most successful crew that the school ever put in the water. His friend, Richard Spender, wrote that Roger was always remarkable for his perfectly natural and cheerful readiness to help, whether in small or big matters. 'This was all the more to his credit because his nature was in some ways rather sensitive, and he appreciated the various difficulties which arose in a rowing club. His unfailing good temper and good sportsmanship helped us to meet all the vagaries of fortune.' He won the trophy for the Brickwood Sculls three years in succession, and returned it for further competition, although tradition entitled him to keep it. It continues to remain on display in Big School. Roger had the fine physique and long reach that made the good oarsman, plus a natural instinct for leadership – he was Captain of Boats – which inspired all those under him.

'Towards other younger and less experienced boys,' his friend Richard wrote, 'he was always considerate and sympathetic. Always a good companion, he entered into the humorous side of life in a club with great enjoyment.' During his final leave, he went down to the riverside to see his friends and to learn the news of the Boat Club.

Roger was a great sportsman, as was said of him, 'in the finest sense of the term', and he excelled at rugby and also took a prominent part in many other sporting activities, winning sixteen cups and eight medals. In spite of his success he remained remarkably unassuming, and cared much more about doing his best than about any marks of distinction. He was wing three-quarter in the 1st XV (winning his colours), a member of the Shooting VIII, and Sergeant-at-Arms for the Debating Society, while throwing himself enthusiastically into a number of small parts in numerous productions by the Dramatic Society. It was written later of him that he had been one of the most popular boys at school (often he could be heard playing a ukulele in the Prefect's Study, now the study of the headmaster), a friend to every colleague, and the delight of his schoolmasters. He was the first boy to arrive with speed and noise at school on a motorcycle, and later, the first to arrive by car – an Austin 7. Then, in the summer of 1939, both he and his elder brother John decided to join the Royal Air Force – John went to fly Wellington bombers with 149 Squadron at RAF Mildenhall, and finally Roger arrived at Middle Wallop to fly Spitfires with 609 Squadron on 11 June.

He was very soon in action as wave after wave of attacks on the airfields of Southern England was launched. Spitfires, Hurricanes and Messerschmitts wheeled, arched, dived and strafed each other in the dramatic dogfights on which Britain's survival at this point depended.

Flight Sergeant 'Titch' Groves, one of the ground crew with 609 Squadron, kept a diary that includes many references to Roger's activities:

609 Squadron duty board.

609 Squadron pursue a Heinkel.

609 group at Middle Wallop.

Taken by Rogers Miller's Spitfire gun camera.

13 July – Flying Officer Dundas R6634, Pilot Officer Overton L1082 and Pilot Officer Miller L1065 were detailed to patrol a convoy. They didn't find the convoy but got mixed up in a nice air battle. Plt Off Miller damaged a Dornier and a Me 110. It was later confirmed that the Dornier damaged by Pilot Officer Miller was in fact shot down.

12 August – Air battle over Portland and Swanage. The day's bag: [included] Pilot Officer Miller R6915 Me 110.

30 August – Practice at quick scramble by 'A' Flight. Pilot Officer Miller L1096 was so eager to do his best, didn't wait for the starter trolley to be pulled clear, turned and damaged his rudder on it. New rudder required.

24 September – Enemy raids seemed now to concentrate on the South Coast and the squadron was involved in one over Swanage. Pilot Officer Miller (Yellow 3) X4107 recorded a Dornier 17 damaged and crashed south of the Isle of Wight.

25 September – Another raid on Swanage. Plt Officer Miller X4107, in command of Yellow Section, led the attack on fifteen Me 110s which were circling at 23,000 feet, Heinkel He III destroyed and given credit with another pilot of half another.

Groves also recorded the events of 27 September, but a more detailed account appears in the operations record book of the squadron and in the published memories of David Crook and Chris Goss.

A large group of about sixty bombers, escorted in force by fighters, was on the way to bomb Bristol, and shortly before noon, 609 Squadron was scrambled to intercept. However, the controller placed them in a hopeless position for a successful interception, and the Germans had dropped their bombs and were forming a wide circle and heading south. Not being able to assume an advantageous position of attack, what with the fighters lurking above, 609 did not go into action, but neither were the Messerschmitts keen to pounce, despite considerable advantage of height. Roger Miller, flying his Spitfire, decorated with a greyhound with the word 'Mick' underneath (named after the famous greyhound 'Mick the Miller'), was in command of 'B' flight and spotted fifteen Me 110s circling in the area between Warmwell and Blandford Forum at about 27,000 feet, and led the squadron in to attack.

Flying Officer Dundas remembered: 'We climbed around them, then dived into the middle of the circle. I saw Yellow One (Roger) collide with a Messerschmitt

110 while executing a beam attack. The Messerschmitt turned out to get his cannon working on Mick and they hit head on. There was a terrific explosion, a sheet of flame and a column of black smoke. I glimpsed a Spitfire's wing fluttering out and the white of a parachute with something on the end. It was ghastly.'

David Crook wrote: 'I was flying behind Mick and he turned slightly left to attack a 110 which was coming towards him. But the German was as determined as Mick and refused to give way or alter course to avoid this head-on attack. Their

Dole Ash Farm.

aggregate closing speed was at least 600 mph and an instant later they collided. There was a terrific explosion and many little fragments fluttered down and that was all.'

The pilot of the Messerschmitt, Gefreiter Georg Jackstadt, although wounded, managed to parachute from his disintegrating plane (this was the parachute with 'something on the end' recalled by Dundas) and was captured. His radio operator was still in the remains of the fighter when it crashed at Piddletrenthide, 8 miles from Dorchester. Roger had been killed instantly, and his body was found in what remained of his Spitfire at Doles Ash Farm on the Downs. David Crook recalls walking to a late lunch that Friday afternoon and sitting at the very table where at breakfast, only a few hours before, 'I had sat next to Mick, but only this time he was lying dead in a Dorsetshire field.'

In a letter to Roger's parents, his commanding officer wrote: 'During the time that I have been in command of the squadron I have had ample opportunity of judging your son's excellent qualities as an officer and as a pilot. He was unfailingly cheerful in all circumstances and we all feel his loss very much indeed and extend our sympathies to you and your family.'

The *Stratford-upon-Avon Herald* report noted that he was, 'One of the few, as the Prime Minister has said, to whom so much is owed by so many – yet the people of Stratford remember him as a schoolboy only last year. He was a charming personality, and he will be mourned by a host of friends.'

One of Roger's friends wrote: 'Great as is our sense of loss, we who knew him cannot fail to be very grateful for having been privileged to be his friend and very proud of his fine record of unselfish service.'

It was a cruel loss for his parents, who only six weeks earlier had lost their other son John when his Wellington bomber crashed. They were a well-known and greatly respected family.

Roger's service at Perry Bar was conducted by the Reverend J.E. Hughes of Radford Semele and assisted by the Reverend Cecil Knight, Headmaster of King Edward VI School. The Garland Miller Family formed a strong friendship with the Thornley family of Radford Semele, and both families spent much of their time at Radford Hall, coming to see the village as their spiritual home. A younger Miller daughter, Rebecca, had died aged eight months, and was buried in the churchyard of St Nicholas Church in Radford Semele, and the ashes of her two brothers were buried near to their sister.

In July 1941, the Air Ministry informed Roger's parents that he had been posthumously awarded a certificate of mention in dispatches from Air Chief Marshal Sir Hugh Dowding for gallant and distinguished services.

For very many years, at the Battle of Britain Thanksgiving Service, held in the Guild Chapel in Stratford-upon-Avon and conducted by the Chaplain of the Stratford Branch of the Aircrew Association, Roger was remembered by name.

He is commemorated on the Alveston War Memorial, on the KES Boat Club Memorial in the Garden of Remembrance, and in the Memorial Library at King Edward VI School.

> *Now you have sped into the Sun,*
> *And stand ennobled in proud robes of flame.*
> *We can no longer see you,*
> *For the light that clothes you is too fine a fire*
> *For our dull, ordinary eyes.*
> *But every day we shall remember you*
> *In the brave glory of the golden sun.*
> Richard Spender,
> to R.G.M. (Fighter-Pilot, killed in action, 1940)

Notes

1. In 2006, during a visit to the school archive, Rogers' sister Sally presented all the cups and medals that her brother had won at KES, and also the camera that he had carried with him very often in his Spitfire.

2. The Brickwood Sculls Trophy was presented in 1928 by Sir John and Lady Brickwood as a prize for rowing. In 2011, the Brickwood Cup for Open Sculls was reintroduced in memory of Rogers Miller during the annual rowing on Benefactors' Day, and was presented by his niece, and Sally's daughter, Carey Parkinson.

3. Spitfire R6915, flown by Rogers Miller on 12 August 1940, is on display in the atrium of the Imperial War Museum in London. Following a visit to see his brother John at RAF Mildenhall, Roger had flown low over the family farm at Alveston and the Boat Club on the Avon – well remembered by Bill Collins, who was down by the river being coached to cox by Richard Spender.

Chapter 9

ROBERT HOLDER

Sergeant, Pilot, 151 Squadron, Royal New Zealand Air Force
26 October 1940

Though the world has slipped and gone,
Sounds my loud discordant cry
Like the steel birds' song on high.
Edith Sitwell, *Lullaby*, 1940

There is an old quatrain that commemorates the villages where tradition has it that William Shakespeare, an Old Boy of King Edward VI School, had drunk a horn or more of ale:

Piping Pebworth, dancing Marston,
Haunted Hilborough, hungry Gratton,
Dodging Exhall, Papist Wixford,
Beggarly Broom and drunken Bidford.

Across the fields south-west and 7 miles downstream from Stratford-upon-Avon, Bidford-on-Avon grew around an ancient ford, now a narrow fifteenth-century stone bridge. Robert Holder was born in April 1917 in Bidford-on-Avon, where his father was a market gardener. Privately educated at Weston College in Weston-super-Mare, he returned to Bidford when his father died and arrived at King Edward VI School in June 1933. He remained there until January 1934. He played for the 1st XV and gained his 2nd XV colours. On leaving school he worked for a poultry farmer in Broom, a small hamlet close to Bidford-on-Avon, on the banks of the river Arrow that meanders into the Avon.

Deciding on a career in farming, in January 1938, at the age of twenty-one Robert emigrated to New Zealand, where he became a farming cadet at Waitangirua, below Motu Falls, near Gisborne, where Captain Cook had landed in October 1769. The following January he applied unsuccessfully for a short service commission in the Royal New Zealand Air Force, but with the declaration of war in Europe he volunteered for aircrew and was accepted. Selected for pilot training, he reported to the Royal New Zealand Air Force (RNZAF) Ground

Training School at Weraroa, north of Wellington, on 19 November 1939.

Weraroa was the first training school for all New Zealand entrants to the RNZAF, and through the Royal New Zealand Air Force to the Royal Air Force. There was ground training – administration, airmanship, air navigation, mathematics, parachutes, reconnaissance, RAF law and discipline, and signals – a total of six weeks before 'passing out' followed by a posting for further training. On 18 December, Robert was sent for elementary flying to No. 2 Empire Flying Training School at New Plymouth, on the west coast of North Island, where the instructors were all ex-aero club pilots. Flying Gypsy Moths DH60 and DH82, he flew solo for the first time on 8 January 1940, and following sixty hours flying training he was posted to No. 2 Flying Training School at Woodbourne in South Island. Continuing to train in

Robert Holder.

Vickers Vincents, Robert was awarded his wings in June 1940 and promoted to sergeant.

Completing an advanced flying programme, Robert boarded the troopship RMS *Rangitane* on 12 July for the return to his homeland. On arrival, following a short induction course at Uxbridge in late August, he was posted to No. 6 Operational Training Unit based at Sutton Bridge, on the border of Cambridge and Norfolk, near The Wash, on 11 September 1940, to train on the Miles M9 Master monoplane and particularly Hurricanes.

On 30 September, he arrived at RAF Digby, 12 miles south of Lincoln, as a replacement pilot for 151 Squadron, where the unit was recovering from severe losses sustained during the Battle of Britain. The squadron had converted to night fighting and they were on 'readiness' during this time, so Hurricanes were regularly scrambled to investigate reports of German raiders.

On the voyage over to Britain on RMS *Rangitane*, Robert had become close friends with a New Zealand pilot, Douglas Stanley, who had also been posted to 151 Squadron. Just after 8.30 pm on 26 October, both of them were engaged in night flying circuits and landings at Colby Grange in Lincolnshire. While waiting his turn at the end of the runway, he saw Sergeant Douglas Stanley take off in a Hurricane Mk I and crash 500 yards beyond the airfield boundary.

Robert was immediately asked by his flight commander if he felt fit enough to carry on, and that under the circumstances he would understand if Robert cancelled the exercise. He replied: 'Affirmative,' electing to carry on. As rescuers were

Robert Holder's grave at Bidford-on-Avon.

Bidford-on-Avon war memorial.

fighting the flames of the blazing Hurricane in order to remove Stanley's body, Robert took off in his Hurricane and, seconds later, entered a steep left-hand turn and flew at full throttle into the ground 800 yards beyond his friend's burning plane.

Douglas Stanley was buried in the Station Churchyard at Scopwick in Lincolnshire and Robert Holder was laid to rest in Bidford-on-Avon. Each year on Remembrance Day, flowers are placed on his grave.

Robert is remembered each year at the reunion of 151 Squadron held in the Falcon Hotel in Stratford-upon-Avon, and is commemorated on the Bidford-on-Avon War Memorial and in the Memorial Library at King Edward VI School.

> *So we must laugh and drink from the*
> *deep blue cup of the sky.*
> John Masefield, *Laugh and be Merry*

Notes
1. RMS *Rangitane* was attacked by the German surface raiders *Orion* and *Komet* 300 miles off the coast of New Zealand and sunk on 27 November 1940. Of the 500 on board, sixteen were killed; the survivors were imprisoned for three weeks and then released on the island of Emirau in New Guinea. One hundred and fifty of the men were transported back to Germany and to prisoner of war camps.

Chapter 10

STANLEY RICHARD PHILLIPS

Leading Aircraftsman Cadet,
Royal Air Force Volunteer Reserve
12 December 1940

They that have climbed the white mists of the morning,
They that have soared, before the world's awake
John Gillespie Magee, *Per Adua*

Primarily an observation and light bomber, the Hawker Audax was developed as a trainer for all the major aircraft that were in service with the Royal Air Force. First flown in 1932, it was used as a variant of the Hawker Hart for a co-operation role with the Army. Powered by a 225hp Rolls-Royce Kestral IB engine, the standard version resembled the Hawker Hart, but had exhaust pipes extending to mid-fuselage on both sides. Twenty-nine-and-a-half feet in length and with two crew, the Audax had a maximum speed of 170mph.

Several of the Audax were used for training at Ansty Airfield, near Coventry. Planned as a flying school by Air Service Training Limited of Hamble in Hampshire, the land near Whitley had been acquired by Armstrong Siddeley in January 1936 and was converted for training on 3 September 1939.

By July 1940, when Stanley Phillips joined the Royal Air Force, the Germans occupied most of Western Europe. Swift and successful campaigns in the Low Countries, Belgium and France had been followed by rapid victories in Denmark and Norway. Throughout August and September, the German Air Force had attempted to seize control of the skies over Southern England as a prelude to invasion. Harbour and shipping were their main targets. The Luftwaffe pilots were confident – with good cause, as they had swept the skies of their enemies in all campaigns so far. What they did not realize was that one of their principal weapons, surprise, had been lost. Decoded signals revealed their plans and Britain's radar system (Radio Direction Finding – RDF) quickly picked up approaching aircraft. So, failing to achieve control of the skies, the Germans had begun a campaign of day and night bombing of British cities. They had seriously underestimated the talented and resilient pilots of the Royal Air Force. This combination of amateurs and professionals had respect for each other. They were mainly reservists who had

Stanley Phillips.

attained a very high degree of skill, could think for themselves and were able to devise new tactics day by day. Several of Stanley's school friends were in the RAF; he had known the Miller brothers, played in the 1st XV with Standish Mottram, and Philip Tyler had been a colleague at work, so, aged twenty-four, he elected to train as a pilot.

Stanley Phillips arrived at King Edward VI School in June 1928, having attended the Crypt School in Gloucester and earning a scholarship from the Gloucestershire County Council. He became a member of the 1st XV ('possessing a remarkable turn of speed') and was awarded 2nd XV colours. Leaving school in December 1932 and gaining the Oxford School Certificate with honours, he crossed Church Street to begin a career with the National Farmers' Union Mutual Insurance. Always enjoying sport, Stanley played hockey in Stratford and became a regular and popular member of the NFU cricket team. It is likely that he would have happily remained at the offices in Church Street for many years had it not been for the outbreak of war and the subsequent loss of many friends.

On Thursday 12 December 1940, during a training flight in Audax K7445, Phillips was killed when the aeroplane hit the cable of a balloon and crashed to the ground, bursting into flames. Stanley's friends at the NFU, who he had visited just a week earlier, were strongly represented at his funeral service, which was held at Holy Trinity Church on Tuesday, 17 December and conducted by Canon Noel Prentice, assisted by the headmaster of King Edward VI School, the Reverend

Cecil Knight. Draped with the Union flag, the coffin was carried by four of his friends from the NFU, and the burial at Stratford-upon-Avon cemetery was also attended by prefects and Old Boys of his school.

Stanley Phillips is commemorated on the NFU Mutual War Memorial at the head offices in Tiddington, on the memorial in Holy Trinity Church, on the plaques in the Garden of Remembrance in Old Town, and in the Memorial Library at King Edward VI School.

> *They knew hope's blossom, not its bitter fruit,*
> *Nor aught of life except that life was good.*
> A.P. Herbert, *The Secret Battle*

Notes

1. The only Hawker Audax believed to still exist is owned by Aero Vintage in Rye, Sussex.

Stanley Phillips' grave in Stratford Cemetery.

Chapter 11

EDWARD MALCOLM KENNARD

Apprentice Merchant Seaman,
23 February 1941

There are no roses on a sailor's grave
No lilies on an ocean wave
The only tribute is the seagull's sweeps
And the teardrops that a sweetheart weeps.
Naval song

In August 1939, the Royal Navy took up war stations and the Government decided to introduce convoys along the east coast of Britain to prevent a breakout by the German fleet into the Atlantic. Ocean shipping, however, would sail alone until the Germans showed their hand. The invasion of Norway in April, and of France in June 1940, meant that the Germans could circumvent any British blockade and reach into the Atlantic. The Germans had played their hand, creating a thorough reappraisal by the British of their naval strategy. By the end of the First World War they had learned a great deal about effectively defeating submarines, but by 1939, much of this had been forgotten. So what Winston Churchill was to call the 'Battle of the Atlantic' was, he knew, the Battle for Britain. Very much dependent on imported goods, Britain required in excess of 1 million tons of imported material each week in order to fight and survive a war.

An already bad situation changed for the worse once the Germans occupied France in 1940. This gave the Germans bases on the French coast that shortened the journey to the operational area, and multiplied their effectiveness. In addition, the Germans deployed Focke-Wulf Fw 200 Kondors for reconnaissance. They had a range of 2,206 miles and could locate a convoy and radio its position to the U-boats. The Germans were able to keep fifteen submarines, called a Wolf Pack, operating in the Atlantic at any one time. Stationed singly, several miles apart in a patrol position, they waited to observe the convoy. It was very effective.

Britain had much faith in Anti-Submarine Detection Investigate Committee (ASDIC), which consisted of an underwater directional sound transmitter and receiver. If the transmissions encountered a submarine, a series of 'pinging' signals accurately detected its distance and direction, but it could not remain in contact throughout an attack, and was totally ineffective when a U-boat was on the surface.

German U-boat commanders called the period between July and October 1940 the 'Happy Time'. An ocean convoy could consist of an oblong of ships proceeding slowly sideways across the Atlantic. For example, a fifty-ship convoy consisted of ten columns, each of five ships in line. It often proved an awkward formation in bad weather, particularly when westbound against a prevailing wind. It was also necessary to zigzag. Fifty ships in close company needed to alter course by the clock several times each hour. Once the escort vessels left the convoy at its dispersal point, lone ships that fell behind were picked off by the waiting U-boats. During these four months,

Malcolm Kennard.

217 merchant ships were sunk. Mass attacks by Wolf Packs caught convoy escorts unprepared, and apart from the ineffectiveness of ASDIC against U-boats on the surface, there was no proper communication between escort vessels other than signal lamps using Morse code, sirens and flags. Escort commanders did not know each other and had not been briefed on tactics.

Admiral Sir Percy Noble, Commander-in-Chief, Western Approaches, said: 'They know, these men, that the Battle of the Atlantic means wind and weather, cold and strain and fatigue, all in the face of a host of enemy craft above and below, awaiting the specific moment to send them to death. They have not even the mental relief of hoping for an enemy humane enough to rescue.' The 30,000 men of the British Merchant Navy who fell victim to the U-boats between 1939 and 1945, the majority drowned or killed by exposure on the cruel North Atlantic Sea, were quite as certainly front-line warriors as the soldiers and fighter pilots to whom they ferried the necessities of combat. If sixty ships left Canada, perhaps twenty to twenty-five arrived in the United Kingdom. The Merchant Navy had an overall death rate of 19 per cent, far higher than any of the armed forces. Saluting the bravery and sacrifice of these men, Admiral Sir Percy Noble observed: 'To cross that ocean in a slow-moving merchant ship was to walk hand in hand with death for every minute of the day and night.'

The Kennard family were long established builders in Stratford-upon-Avon (their old painted sign can still be seen on a wall in Ryland Street), and an uncle was the local manager of the Warwickshire and Worcestershire Building Society.

A great enthusiast of model railways, Malcolm was just ten years and three months old when he joined King Edward VI School in September 1934. Although he always remained the youngest boy in his year, he was known for his gaiety and courage, and grew to be physically strong, becoming a member of the 1st XV and gaining his 1st IV colours with a crew captained by Richard Spender in 1940.

Just past his sixteenth birthday, Malcolm left school in November 1940 – no longer a boy, not yet a man – and joined the Merchant Navy, where seamen were allowed to go to sea at sixteen rather than eighteen for the Royal Navy. Full of adventure, he was one of those who possessed what Rupert Brooke had called 'with Splendid Hearts'.

He joined SS *Temple Moat*, a 4,400-ton steamer, built in 1928 and with a crew of thirty-six. The usual cargo was coal, and she was a regular member of the Atlantic convoy. Although this period was still the 'Happy Time' for the U-boats,

SS Temple Moat.

The end of SS Temple Moat.

bad weather in January in the Western Approaches kept the number of sinkings down. However, on 5 January 1941, when south of Iceland, SS *Temple Moat* was damaged by bombs and gunfire from a Focke-Wulf Kondor aircraft.

Convoy OB 288 left Liverpool on Tuesday, 18 February 1941. Amongst the forty-six ships was SS *Temple Moat* (Master: Thomas Ludlow MBE) with a cargo of coal bound for Buenos Aires. One day later, *U-95*, commanded by Gerd Schreiber, left its base at Lorient in Brittany for operation in the North Atlantic.

On Saturday, 22 February, the order was given for the convoy to disperse. Having located the convoy, a pack of U-boats was waiting. Unable to maintain speed due to engine problems, SS *Temple Moat* fell behind, and at 1.45 am on Sunday morning, 23 February, she was hit by one torpedo from *U-95* and sank very quickly by the bow, south of Iceland, at 59 degrees 27 minutes north, 20 degrees 20 minutes west. The crew of thirty-six, including two other apprentices, were all lost.

Ten ships were sunk from Convoy OB 288, and German sources indicate that had it not been for torpedo failures, many more ships could have been sunk. *U-95* continued to patrol successfully in the North Atlantic until it was ordered to the

Mediterranean on 22 November 1941. Six days later, it was torpedoed and sunk by a Dutch submarine.

Malcolm Kennard is commemorated on the Tower Hill Memorial, just north of the Tower of London. The memorial is in the form of a sunken garden, and the main inscription reads:

> The twenty-four thousand of the Merchant Navy and Fishing Fleets whose names are honoured on the walls of this garden gave their lives for their country and have no grave but the sea.

He is also commemorated in the Stratford Baptist Church, in the Memorial Library at King Edward VI School, and in the Garden of Remembrance in Old Town.

> *I'm talking of AB's and firemen,*
> *Of stewards and greasers and cooks*
> *Who manned the big steamers in convoy*
> *(You won't read about them in books).*
> Edward Carpenter, Merchant Seaman

Notes
1. During the course of the war, 6.1 per cent of Allied shipping losses were inflicted by surface raiders, and 6.5 per cent by mines, 13.4 per cent were caused by air attack and 70 per cent by U-boats.
2. Malcolm Kennard was the youngest by two years of Old Boys of the school to die in either of the world wars.

Chapter 12

ARTHUR CHARLES NORTH
Sergeant, Observer, 105 Squadron
16 May 1941

sat in this tattered scarecrow of the sky
hearing it cough, the great plane catching
now the first dark clouds upon her wing-base
John Bayliss, *Reported Missing*

The German action against Norway in early April 1940 is considered one of the most daring gambles in the history of naval warfare. Mounted against British naval superiority, almost the entire German surface fleet was committed, and if the Royal Navy had been in the right place at the right time, believed Naval Historian Eric Grove, it might have been destroyed. Due to a series of miscalculations, the Germans succeeded in occupying Norway and thereby securing naval and air bases from which they could operate against Britain.

From RAF Lossiemouth, north of the Cairngorms on the north-east coast of Scotland, Blenheim bombers could attack German shipping off Norway. Taking off in formation, they broke off in pairs as they approached the Norwegian coast, each sweeping a section of sea for a few dangerous minutes before turning hastily for home, whether they had bombed or not, in the hope of anticipating the scrambling Messerschmitts. A crew that ditched on these operations knew that their slender hope of surviving in the Channel was extinguished altogether in the North Sea.

Following training as an observer, Arthur North was posted to 105 Squadron at RAF Lossiemouth, where he 'crewed up' with Pilot Officer Richard Alban Richards from Herefordshire and Wireless Operator/Gunner Ernest Edmund Snutch from Leicestershire to fly a Blenheim Mk IV. The Blenheim bomber had suffered appalling losses against targets in Germany, France and the Low Countries, and against shipping in the North Sea – so much so that the Prime Minister had written of their futile sacrifice that: 'The Charge of the Light Brigade at Balaclava is eclipsed in brightness by these almost daily deeds of fame.'

In the early months of the war, 105 Squadron had served in France and had attacked the Meuse bridges in an attempt to halt the German advance. On its return to Britain it was re-formed at Lossiemouth and continued coastal sweeps off Norway. On Friday, 16 May 1941, Blenheim Mk IV T2118 was ordered on a anti-shipping sortie in the Norwegian fjords. Daniel Swift wrote of the time spent by aircrew before a flight: 'You go out to the plane and sit on the grass, and smoke. You know that you will have no real food for ten hours. You have a thermos of tea and a piece of chocolate, but it will be so cold in the plane that you have to hold the chocolate in your mouth to warm it up. It will feel like -50 degrees and your teeth will ache, and so you get dressed up. Uniform, then a woolly, a thick jumper, then a fur-lined flying suit, with zips, so that if you are wounded they can unzip if from your body; on your feet, silk socks, then air force socks, then wool socks, then flying boots.' During the flight across the North Sea the cold was

Arthur North.

appalling, vital systems jammed and limbs seized. Arthur North had lived in Wrexham until his father died, and was at King Edward VI School between 1928 and 1935. 'Always cheerful', he was a solid member of the 1st XV, gained 2nd XV colours, and regularly rowed for the school Boat Club, he left in February 1935 to begin a career in insurance with a broker in Birmingham. You can still take the early morning train on the North Warwickshire Line, as he did each day, from Stratford-upon-Avon, past Henley-in-Arden and Yardley Wood to Birmingham. He had moved to an insurance company in Coventry by the time war was declared, and he joined the Royal Air Force Volunteer Reserve in 1940.

Blenheim Mk IV T2118 took off at 2.30 in the afternoon, for the fjords and Bergen, an old Hanseatic town of tall, gabled wooden warehouses painted in warm barn red. From all over the harbour 'flak hosed up', and T2118 was last seen heading along the fjord at 50 feet, Two days later, his mother received a letter stating: 'The aircraft on which Sergeant North was observer failed to return to its base on Friday, after an operational flight, but this does not necessarily mean that he is killed or wounded.' His mother and sister continued to hope for good news, until in early September they were informed that he had been killed in action. 'Further information received from the Norwegian Red Cross Society states that he was shot down near Bergen.'

The *Stratford-upon-Avon Herald* reported: 'The passing of this young airman – another of that fine band of youth to which this country owes so much – will bring sorrow to his many friends.' Wherever possible a crew who died together were buried together. Both Pilot Officer Alban Richards and Sergeant Arthur North were buried in the Bergen (Mollendal) Church Cemetery. The body of Sergeant Ernest Snutch was never found and he has no known grave.

Arthur North is commemorated in the Garden of Remembrance by Holy Trinity Church and in the Memorial Library at King Edward VI School.

This was their kingdom, the air, and it bore them like kings,
And they were the shield for us all who dwelt under their wings.
Edward Shanks, *Triumphant Threnody*

Chapter 13

JAMES OVERBURY

Trooper, Warwickshire Yeomanry
19 May 1941

The fighting man shall from the sun
Take warmth, and life from the glowing earth
Julian Grenfell, *Into Battle*

T he armistice between France and Germany in June 1940 divided France into two zones, the north came under German military occupation, and the south was governed by the French from the spa town of Vichy in the Auvergne. The legitimacy of Vichy France was challenged by General Charles de Gaulle, who claimed to represent the legitimate and Free French government. Wishing to prevent Vichy from agreeing to German demands to move war supplies through French territories in North Africa, and to establish air bases in French-controlled Syria as major springboards for attacks on Egypt, the Allies planned an offensive against Vichy forces in the region.

At the beginning of May 1941, Vichy France signed the 'Paris Protocols', granting the Germans access to military facilities in Syria, and allowing German and Italian planes to refuel in Syria. This was seen by the British as a direct threat to strategic oil supplies and communications, and they sent a large force under the command of General Sir Henry 'Jumbo' Maitland Wilson, General Officer Commanding, Palestine and Trans-Jordon. In the inter-war years he had played a leading role in the revolutionary concept of motorized infantry battalions working alongside tanks.

The Vichy French fought with great courage and determination and, after the first week, an attack heading towards Damascus had started well enough and the important bridge near Tel Shehab had been secured. It was important that this success would pave the way for entry into the Syrian capital by a Free French force, because Britain was anxious to show that the campaign was not about an old imperial rival exploiting the misfortunes of France. *TIME* magazine referred to the fighting as 'a mixed show' and reported that: 'the British-Free French drive for Vichy-held Syria [was] a weird combination of Blitz and bicker, glad-handing and heavy punching, pushover and furious resistance.'

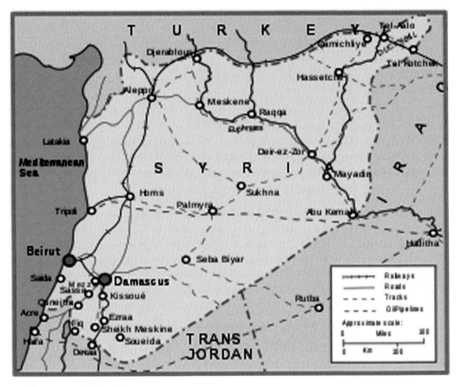

Battles against Vichy France.

Nineteen-year-old James Overbury became a Trooper in the Warwickshire Yeomanry, part of the 6th Cavalry Brigade in 1936. Mobilized at the Drill Hall in Stratford-upon-Avon on 2 September 1939, the Yeomanry was the only British cavalry division (with horses) during the Second World War and were sent to the Middle East in January 1940 as a garrison and occupation force. England owed a great deal to its yeomen. These placid, sturdy men of the shires had for generations worked and lived for the land. The yeomen of yesterday went to war to defend their land with their bows, their pikes and their muskets.

The 6th Cavalry Brigade had disembarked at Haifa in heavy rain on 9 January 1940. Boarding buses – the horses were loaded onto open rail trucks – they travelled to Afula on the Plain of Esdraelon. Again in heavy rain, the regiment left Afula on 27 January for Tiberias and Rosh Pinna, before moving into the centre of Tiberias on the shores of the Sea of Galilee. Bad weather continued and on 21 March, they moved again, this time to Rosh Pinna Camp.

Following the capitulation of France on 24 June and the entry of Italy into the war on Germany's side, patrols were intensified along the frontiers, especially following a number of Italian air raids over Palestine.

In early October, the regiment moved to the coastal area at Karkur Camp, and just before Christmas they took part in an extensive series of exercises by the river Jordan, before returning, once again in pouring rain, to Karkur.

In the early New Year there were vehicle driving and maintenance courses, before the regiment moved to Nablus on 18 March and transferred to 4th Cavalry Brigade. D Squadron (with Trooper Overbury) arrived at Allenby Barracks in Jerusalem. The 6th Cavalry Brigade, together with a battalion of infantry from the Essex Regiment, a mechanized regiment of the Arab Legion (the regular army of Trans-Jordan) and supporting artillery, was reorganized as the unromantic and strictly functional HABFORCE for operations in Iraq, including the relief of the base at RAF Habbaniya and the occupation of Baghdad. The yeoman's role was that of lorried infantry equipped with Morris 15cwt CS8 trucks. By now almost all the horses had gone, and the regiment. Paul Baker wrote in *Yeoman Yeoman* that, although there was regret over the loss of the horses, 'it was soon found that drivers developed a kind of feeling for their new charges, and miracles of improvisation were achieved to keep the uncomfortable old trucks in a state of readiness.'

Armoured car in HABFORCE, Palestine. Warwickshire Yeomanry

In April 1941, four army officers, encouraged by Germany, led a revolt in Iraq against the pro-British Regent, and attacked the RAF base at Habbaniya. The main reason for the Allied force in the region was to secure the oil pipelines intact, as the Middle East was vital to the British.

German interest in the region was part of their plan to seize oil reserves and to secure the area before the invasion of Russia on 22 June 1941, when more than 3 million men, 600,000 vehicles and 3,350 tanks were massed along a 1,250-mile frontier from the Baltic to the Black Sea. 'When Operation *Barbarossa* is launched,' declared Hitler, 'the world will hold its breath.'

The rebels were known to be in the fort at the H2 Pumping Station on the vital oil pipeline, and at 9.30 on the morning of 19 May, D Squadron of the Warwickshire Yeomanry went into action. Getting as near as possible to the south side of the station, they gained the attention of the defenders by their rapid fire. As the morning progressed and the sun rose higher in the sky, the men were subjected to the hot wind of 110 degrees Fahrenheit as they held out in the open. It was a gruelling experience, and it was during this time and under heavy enemy fire that James Overbury was killed.

Late in the afternoon the oil storage tanks were set on fire, and under cover of the smoke a detachment of D Squadron – with members of the Arab Legion – burst into the station and drove out the enemy force. The small number remaining in the fort waved a white flag and capitulated. Paul Barker wrote that the swift action of the British forces forestalled the German aspirations in the region.

James Overbury was buried in the Commonwealth War Cemetery in Syria. He is commemorated on the Wellesbourne War Memorial and in the Memorial Library at King Edward VI School.

> *Yeoman, Yeoman, why do you roam*
> *Yeoman, Yeoman, so far from home*
> *Yeoman, Yeoman, why do you stray?*
> Anonymous Yeoman

Chapter 14

GEORGE EDWARD PRINT

Leading Seaman, HM Submarine, Royal Navy
23 August 1941

knew it was finished, looking at the sea
which shone back patterns in kaleidoscope
knew that their shadow would meet them by the way,
close and catch at them, drown their single hope:
John Bayliss, *Reported Missing*

It takes a particular type of man to choose to volunteer to become a submariner. Perhaps an adventurer, certainly someone with no aversion to enclosed spaces, and who is able and prepared to spend hours, sometimes days, deep below the waves. During the Second World War even the largest of submarines were small, with severe limitations on space, accommodation and facilities. Food deteriorated, fresh water was rationed, and the air was often cold and damp. A submariner's pay was modest, although higher than other ranks in the Royal Navy and Merchant Navy. Entering the imagination in the fifteenth century, submersibles first appeared in reality in 1620, and as a weapon in the war of American Independence. By 1914, Jules Verne had written of the fictional *Nautilus*, powered by electricity provided by sodium/mercury batteries, and Germany had assembled a flotilla of U-boats that subsequently sunk 5,000 Allied ships during the First World War.

Built by Vickers Armstrong in Barrow-in-Furness in 1940, HMS P32 was one of the few submarines that used the Pennant number and was not given a name. At 191 feet in length and capable of a surface speed of 11.25 knots and a submerged speed of 10 knots, P32 was launched on 15 December 1940, and following trials was sent to join the 10th Submarine Flotilla in Malta.

When in 1940 France agreed an armistice, Italy declared war on Britain and islands in the Eastern Mediterranean fell into German occupation, it was vital for Britain's desert forces based in Egypt to defend the Suez Canal. The situation there became acute when, when following early successes against the Italian Army, they were faced with far more serious opposition by the arrival of the German Afrika Korps. Moreover, whilst the German supplies could cross the Mediterranean to

Libya and Tunisia, Britain's support and reinforcement had to travel around the Cape of Good Hope.

In order to frustrate the German supplies from Italy, the island of Malta was established as a base and an offensive outpost from where to attack the convoy routes to North Africa. Between January 1941 and April 1942, twenty submarines were based at Malta for anti-shipping patrols in the deep waters off Southern Italy. In two respects, the Mediterranean proved a difficult hunting ground for submarines, because the water is deep and clear, thereby making a submerged submarine visible for many miles, and also, in areas, the sea was both shallow and poorly charted. However, much more success was achieved in the shallower waters along the North African coast. There were difficulties here too, because in the shallower waters a great number of mines were laid.

There was ferocious German action against Malta during the early months of 1941, with air raids and low-level minelaying, although the submarine base escaped damage.

George Print received a Governor's Grant to attend King Edward VI School, which he attended between September 1920 and April 1924. He lived in Bull Street in a quiet area of Old Town, and his father worked at Lucy's Mill by the river Avon. His friends at school, Tom Palmer, William Stiles and Thomas Hiatt, were all to die during the Second World War. Leaving school when he was fifteen years old, George became a cadet in the Royal Navy. During the next fourteen years, he rose to the rank of leading seaman, married Lily, had a daughter Marian, and by 1940 had volunteered for submarine service and been posted to His Majesty's Ship P32, arriving in Malta in December.

During an early patrol in April, P32 torpedoed and sank the Italian merchant ship *Barbarigo* off Pantellaria Island in the Strait of Sicily. Leaving Malta on Tuesday, 12 August, P32, with P33 and HMS *Unique*, were ordered to intercept an Italian convoy bound for Libya. Sighting the convoy of five merchant ships, escorted by three Italian destroyers and three patrol craft that were heading to the channel approach to Tripoli Harbour, which had been swept of mines, P32 dived under a moored minefield in an attempt to gain a better attacking position. Believing that he had cleared the mines, the commanding officer, Lieutenant David Abdy, ordered the submarine to periscope depth in order to check the position of the convoy. A mine, either a part of the minefield or one laid by a British aircraft, exploded against the submarine's port side, flooding the boat forward of the control room and killing eight crew members. The explosion put out all the lights, the boat took on a heavy list and sank 210 feet to the bottom. The remaining twenty-four crew moved aft, and Abdy decided that the engine room offered a brighter prospect for escape, but taking into consideration the number of crew members and the time that the submarine had been submerged, plus the pressure being put on the forward control room door, he split the group into two. The coxswain, Petty Officer Kirk

Submarine P32.

P32 conning tower.

and Seaman E. Martin, volunteered to join Abdy in the attempt at a more dangerous escape by the conning tower. Martin was dead on his arrival at the surface, but Abdy and Kirk were picked up by an Italian naval vessel and made prisoners of war. The Italian ship remained at the site for several hours, but there were no other survivors.

In 1999, a Libyan fisher lost his net, which was snagged on the bottom of the sea. Later, a team of professional Libyan divers led by Mohamed Arebi discovered the wreck of P32 covered in nets and standing on its hull at a 45 degree angle to its port side. The engine hatch was open, with the ladder still in place to the open hatch, suggesting an attempt to escape. The understanding that an iron bar was welded over the escape hatch – because it was believed to be a weak point during heavy depth-charging – proved to be wrong in this case.

The *Stratford-upon-Avon Herald* on 20 February 1942 reported that George was missing, and in the edition of 24 August 1945, his wife, and his mother and father, placed an In Memoriam for him. George Print, a keen and successful sportsman who enjoyed playing football and hockey, is commemorated on the Chatham Naval Memorial, in the Garden of Remembrance in Old Town, and in the Memorial Library at King Edward VI School.

> *The time will come when Ocean shall resume*
> *His ancient soveranty upon this isle,*
> *When all our glories shall deep-plunged be*
> *Under a lonely sea.*
> Edward Shanks, *Battle*

Chapter 15

RICHARD FRANK BURNET
TURNER

Ordinary Seaman, Royal Naval Volunteer Reserve
27 September 1941

Peace washes silent o'er the ocean bed,
It sweeps both time and substance in its path.
The years roll forward, pass and make no scar
Upon the toll of conflict's aftermath.
A.R. Rodgers, *To Ships and Men and War*

The Stratford-upon-Avon Boat Club was established in the Falcon Hotel, opposite King Edward VI School, in August 1874, by a group of enthusiastic young rowers who wished to compete in their own and neighbouring regattas. By the end of the century, the club had a flourishing boat house, and the years before 1914 were a golden time for rowing on the river Avon. Recovering from the loss of many of its members who were killed during the First World War, there was a major revival as the regattas became both a sporting and a social event, and there were a number of strong crews. In 1926, the King Edward VI Boat Club was founded, and with the enthusiastic support of the headmaster, Cecil Knight – who recognized it as a further way of forging strong traditions and competitiveness in the school – a crew began rowing with the agreement of the Stratford Boat Club. It was a happy association, because several of the boys became members of successful Stratford IVs, one of whom was Richard ('Dick') Turner, who was a member of the Junior Four in 1931 that set up a club record by winning nine events. His father, Frank Turner, was Head of Chemistry at King Edward VI and also helped to coach the School Junior Four, who were all awarded their rowing caps during the summer of 1929. Dick remained at school until completing the Sixth Form and then joined the offices of a chartered accountant in the town.

Meeting and marrying Moira Turner from Lanarkshire, they moved to London. In the first year of the war, when their home was bombed, Dick's wife and daughter moved to Leamington Spa, and as an ordinary seaman – training for a commission

63

– in the Royal Navy, he was posted to HMS *Springbank*, which was lying in Bangor Bay, near Belfast, awaiting instructions for convoy duties.

Constructed for merchant service in 1926, HMS *Springbank* was a new type of fighter catapult ship that in November 1940 had been commissioned into the Royal Navy, and developed to counter the serious threat from German land-based aircraft, particularly Focke-Wulf Kondors. Formidably armed with eight 4-inch guns and two 2-pounder pom-poms, and manned by naval officers and ratings, the ship was fitted with a cordite-powered catapult amidships, mounted with a Fulmer two-seater naval fighter. When threatened by enemy planes, the fighter was catapulted, and unless it was able to make a land fall, the plane would have to ditch in the sea, with the pilot, theoretically, being pulled out of the water.

Richard Turner.

There was also a detachment on board of Grumman Martlets of 804 Squadron.

Life on Atlantic convoys was a matter of slowly increasing strain, strain still mounting towards a crucial point that could not yet be foreseen, and it took its toll of men's nerves and patience. So, following intensive gunnery training the crew was granted two weeks' leave. HMS *Springbank* operated between Liverpool and Gibraltar, and the usual plan was to escort a convoy for three or four days on the outward journey, and then join a homecoming convoy to escort it safely back to the home port. This was the same convoy route, known as 'the graveyard', described in Nicholas Monsarrat's epic novel *The Cruel Sea*.

In August, a voyage all the way to Gibraltar was eventful but successful, and HMS *Springbank* joined the hastily assembled homeward bound Convoy HG73, with twenty-five merchant ships and six escorts. With German observation posts along the Spanish coast, the convoy sailed late in the afternoon of 17 September into the Mediterranean as if bound for Malta. Then, under cover of darkness, they turned back and steamed through the Straits of Gibraltar and into the Atlantic. It did not take long for the Germans to spot them off Cape St Vincent. It started with a single aircraft, possibly an old friend, a four-engine Focke-Wulf reconnaissance plane, which closed in on the convoy from the east and then began to go round them in slow circles, well out of range of any gunfire they could put up. It had happened to them before, and there was little doubt of what the plane was doing – pinpointing the convoy, shadowing it, noting exactly its course and speed, and then reporting back to some authority. The next day, Fulmers were launched to attack the enemy aircraft but without success, and upon returning to Gibraltar, it was found that faulty ammunition had caused all but one of the Fulmers' guns to jam.

Without air cover, the ships in the convoy were sitting ducks as U371 and three Italian submarines shadowed them for several days, while a U-boat Wolf Pack assembled. On the night of 26 September, they moved in; the attacks began and six ships were sunk. The following morning, in pitch dark and a blowing gale, as the convoy was trying to pick up survivors and organize itself into some sort of order, the U-boats struck again, and three further merchants were sunk, including, at 12.20am, HMS *Springbank*. Hit by two torpedoes on the port side, the order was given to abandon ship. Attempting a rescue, a destroyer came alongside, but several members of the crew misjudged their jump and fell into the sea between the two ships. Whether in the explosions, during the attempted rescue, or amongst the chaos of the event, Dick Turner was lost: 'Missing, presumed killed on war service.'

Convoy HG73 was unlucky to have been the subject of attack from three of the most able U-boat commanders of the war. Eight officers and fifty-eight ratings were saved from HMS *Springbank*, and a hastily assembled Admiralty Board of Enquiry reported that the escorts lacked training as a team.

Richard Turner is commemorated on the Chatham Naval Memorial, in the Garden of Remembrance in Stratford-upon-Avon, and in the Memorial Library at King Edward VI School.

> *A quiet hovers here, elsewhere unfound,*
> *And blesses with its touch and precious grace*
> *The scaffold-skeletons of ships and dust of men*
> *Who, unknown, lie in this last resting place.*
> A.R. Rodgers, *To Ships and Men and War*

HMS Springbank.

Chapter 16

LAURENCE GEOFFREY HILLIER
Sergeant, Observer, 235 Squadron
3 November 1941

But at my back I always hear
Time's winged chariot hurrying near
Andrew Marvell, *To His Coy Mistress*

Throughout 1941, an aircraft was lost for every 10 tons of bombs dropped. It became unthinkable to continue operations at this rate of attrition, especially when a report on the performance of Bomber Command (The Butt Report) made it clear that no significant results were being achieved. Especially hard hit had been the Bristol Blenheim Mk IV that had flown patrols over Holland, and during the Battle of Britain had been used for convoy protection and for photographic reconnaissance over the North Sea. One hundred and thirty-eight Blenheims were lost on these low-level shipping and harbour raids, and the shipping campaign was called off in November 1941 because this number of casualties could no longer be justified. The patrol by Blenheim Mk IV Z6144 'S' for Sugar, in which Sergeant (Observer) Laurence Hillier was lost, was in fact the last one.

Lawrence Hillier.

His brother Philip was already at King Edward VI School when Laurence joined in September 1929, and they both moved in December 1931 to Harrow County School in Pinner. Laurence joined the RAFVR. During the 1930s, as the threat of another war became palpable, it became essential to recruit a large reserve of men from civilian life who were willing to sacrifice weekends and holidays. Drawing its numbers from the industrial areas and 'the whole range of secondary school output', the RAFVR was created. The first aim was to recruit some 800 potential pilots a year. By April 1937, the desired intake had been exceeded, and by September 1939, 5,000 young men of the volunteer reserve had undergone

Blenheim.

training as pilots, followed by aircrew, medical, equipment, administrative and technical branches, which formed an invaluable collection of trained manpower.

Philip Hillier was posted to No. 18 Group, 235 Squadron, at RAF Manston, which in February 1940 was equipped with Bristol Blenheims and transferred from Fighter Command to Coastal Command.

Attacks on enemy shipping began in 1941. With great determination, the crews dived through flak and released their bombs from mast-height – so near that damage was frequent from impact with the ship. In June the squadron were sent to RAF Dyce in Aberdeenshire (now Aberdeen Airport), to begin operations along the Norwegian coast. The first British convoy had sailed to Russia on 21 August 1941, the second in September, and the third in October. Normally passing west of Iceland through the Denmark Strait, rounding Northern Norway then turning south for Murmansk or Archangel, they had the air support from Coastal Command's constant watch over German warships.

At 5.39 on the afternoon of Monday, 3 November, 'S' for Sugar, piloted by Pilot Officer H.W. Van Panhuys from Holland, with the air gunner, Sergeant H.A. Cook and Sergeant Laurence Hillier as observer, took off from RAF Dyce for a patrol of the Faroe Islands, north-west of Scotland and lying between Iceland and Norway, to detect U-boats and German destroyers.

The plane was reported missing from the patrol; only Laurence's body was found and was buried in the Bergen (Mollendal) Church Cemetery in Norway. The pilot and air gunner are commemorated on the RAF Memorial at Runnymede. Following the final 'shipping sweeps' on 2 and 3 November, the terrible toll on Blenheim crews, attacking heavily-armed ships in daylight, ended. In all, 590 ships had been attacked, with 207 claimed sunk or badly damaged. In addition, the aircrews very often had to battle fierce headwinds, huge belts of fog, heavy ice formations that endangered the controls, an inability to make only the occasional use of wireless, and utter weariness.

Laurence Hillier, like his brother Philip who was killed seven months later, is commemorated in the Memorial Library at King Edward VI School.

> *You would think the fury of aerial bombardment*
> *Would rouse God to relent*
> Richard Eberhart, *The Fury of Aerial Bombardment*

Notes
1. Bomber Command Blenheims operated for the last time on 17/18 May 1942.

Chapter 17

JOHN MICHAEL WYLEY

Flying Officer, 260 Squadron
27 November 1941

If they die they'll die,
As you should know,
More swiftly, clearly, star defined,
Then you will ever feel.
H.E. Bates, *How Sleep the Brave*

John Wyley.

Those young men who flew, and they were mostly young, were like gods, and many of them were to be immortalized in golden youth. They tended to look different from mere mortals, with their indifference to regulation uniform, and wore roll-neck jumpers, silk scarves, sunglasses and 'Mae West' life vests thrown casually over leather flying jackets. 'The fighter pilot's emotions,' wrote Richard Hillary, 'are those of a duellist: cool, precise and impersonal.' This indifference was reflected in their approach to life: they hoped for a future but they lived for the day. Many had a dazzling indifference to their own fate.

Like many of his friends and contemporaries – Standish Mottram, Richard Spender and Philip Tyler, and other boys of his generation – John Wyley had enjoyed his years at King Edward VI School, and been a member of the 1st XV and the 2nd XI. Leaving for a career in a Stratford bank, he thought by 1939 it seemed obvious that there was to be a European war. As he had always wanted to fly, he joined the local Royal Air Force Volunteer Reserve. Drawing its recruits from industrial areas and grammar schools, the RAFVR was intended to produce 800 pilots a year; in fact, it had 5,000 pilots either fully trained or under training by September 1939. By then the RAFVR had been extended to cover the complete range of aircrew, medical, equipment, administrative and technical branches. Many had earlier joined flying clubs, and paid between half-a-crown and ten shillings to learn to fly.

In 1940, John Wyley was posted to 260 at RAF Castletown, a fighter squadron flying Hurricanes on air defence and convoy patrols over the North of Scotland. Remaining here until April 1941, he was transferred to RAF Drem in East Lothian to prepare for the squadron moving overseas.

In May, 260 Squadron arrived at RAF Takoradi on the Gold Coast (now Ghana), an important staging point for British aircraft destined for Egypt. Takoradi is the largest city closest to the Equator and the Prime Meridian, making the city the most central location on the world map. Following further training, they were transferred to Egypt, becoming operational with Hurricanes for air defence duties over Palestine and the Lebanon from 11 August to safeguard the oil supplies (the area where another school friend, James Overbury, had been killed in May 1941). Among other work they supported the Army fighting in Abyssinia, where the last Italian troops surrendered in November 1941.

These actions had been sideshows compared with the main task of battling the opposing air forces and the enemy's supply system, so by the end of October the squadron was moved for ground attack and escort duties for the campaign in the Western Desert as part of No. 262 Wing. Mobility and good communications were the main recipes for effective air support. These operations were considered very risky, because at times they were flying low near enemy ground defences, of which they had no knowledge, and were subject to intense fire. Their job was to harass the German troops, destroy their supply lines – both road and rail – negate their air and naval forces, and damage the supplies, particularly oil.

John was flying the distinctive Hawker Hurricane Mk 1 (fifty of which featured shark's mouth markings) when on 27 November he took off from LZ 124 (Landing Zone) near Sidi Rezegh, against advanced German artillery positions. John's plane was hit by ground fire, exploded, and was never found. He is commemorated on the El Alamein Memorial in Egypt, in Holy Trinity Church, in the Garden of Remembrance in Old Town, Stratford-upon-Avon, and the Memorial Library at King Edward VI School.

> *Sunward I've climbed, and joined the tumbling mirth*
> *of sun-split cloud – and done a hundred things*
> *You have not dreamed of – wheeled and soared and swung*
> *High in the sunlit silence.*
>
> John Gillespie Magee, *High Flight*

Notes
1. Richard Hillary, a Battle of Britain pilot, was very badly burned when his Spitfire crashed in September 1940. He later wrote the excellent book *The Last Battle,* and was killed during a training flight in 1943.

Chapter 18

ERIC JOHN EVANS

Sub Lieutenant, Malayan Royal Naval Volunteer Reserve
13 February 1942

*I shall never forget ... as long as I live ... the sound of the little children
Call out for their mothers.*
M.J.V. Miller, survivor, HMS *Giang Bee*

The Fish and Anchor inn is in the small village of Littleton in Worcestershire. It has been there for more than ninety years and the countryside around it has remained more or less the same. There is a blackthorn thicket, and in the summer, there and on both sides of a track down the gully towards the inn, large patches of violets and white sweet violets bloom. The dingle on the east side of the track near the bottom of the gully is carpeted with lesser celandines and whitlow grass flowers. In the 1920s, Eric Evans lived at the inn and played in the tracks and lanes, until at the age of ten he was sent as a boarder to King Edward VI School, where he flourished, gaining his Higher School Certificate and the Charles Flower Scholarship when he went on to Jesus College, Oxford. Graduating in 1935, he was accepted into the Police Department of the Customs and Excise Department of the Federal States of Malaya, based in Singapore, which in the 1930s was the cosmopolitan hub of British interests in the peninsula.

Indeed, it was said that if India was the jewel in the imperial crown, Malaya was the industrial diamond. A model economy, its status was achieved from its own resources and its accumulated budget surpluses.

By the summer of 1941, Japanese relations with the Western powers had deteriorated to the point where its leaders decided to launch their plan for a Greater East Asia Co-Prosperity Sphere, and secure the necessary supplies of raw materials to complete the conquest of the Southeast Asian territories controlled by Britain, France, the United States and the Netherlands. Following the attack on the United States Pacific Fleet at Pearl Harbor on 7 December, Japan's Southern Army quickly moved to the attack in Southern Thailand and northern Malaya on 8 December.

Thailand capitulated on 10 December, thereby allowing the Japanese to establish supply lines to its army in Malaya. Deploying tanks in frontal assaults,

Japanese light infantry bypassed British defences using boats and bicycles. Cut off from supply bases in Southern Malaya, with no air cover, and very demoralized, the British forces withdrew to Singapore by 27 January 1942 to prepare for siege.

Undetected by the British, Japanese forces used collapsible boats to cross the Strait to Singapore's north-west coast. By 13 February, the Japanese controlled all of the island except the south-eastern sector, where thousands of refugees, clutching their one permitted suitcase each, were gathering by the harbour and waiting to board ships.

One of these was HMS *Giang Bee*, a Chinese-owned coastal steamer that had been requisitioned and used as a patrol vessel. On 29 and 30 January, she had rescued survivors from the destroyer HMS *Thanet*, which had been sunk three days earlier. Seeing the dangers attached to a ship designated as a war ship in taking civilian passengers, the captain initially refused to accept them but finally allowed more than 300 refugees to board (a survivor believed that there were 350 on board). Most were women, children and the elderly. Her Malayan crew had been ordered ashore in Singapore, so the crew consisted of a handful of Royal Navy Volunteer Reserve personnel, one of whom was Sub Lieutenant Eric Evans.

In his book *Sinister Twilight*, Noel Barber wrote that whilst many of the people who boarded the ship on that night of 12 February were simply individuals desperate to leave a bombed, burning and shattered Singapore, there were strong social dynamics at work amongst the flood of people who had crowded into Singapore in the previous month. This had resulted in groups of friends, extended families and company employees working together to survive and escape by means of staying in groups they trusted and loved.

With four lifeboats – each could carry thirty-two people – HMS *Giang Bee* was one of forty-four ships that left Singapore in loose convoy formation on the night of 12 February.

Following air attacks during the day on 13 February, when HMS *Giang Bee* was approximately 170 miles south of Singapore, two Japanese destroyers approached at high speed, one of them signalling in incomprehensible Morse code. The captain ordered the lowering of the White Ensign and that all women and children should show themselves on deck.

As one of the destroyers sent a launch towards the *Giang Bee*, two Dutch bombers from Sumatra appeared and circled overhead. The destroyers opened fire on the bombers and recalled the launch. There followed what Noel Barber described as 'a long uneasy wait through the day into dusk and night, when the destroyers trained their searchlights on the *Giang Bee*'. At about 7.30 pm, following a signalled instruction from the Japanese for the ship to be abandoned, the captain ordered all women and children to take to the lifeboats – fifty or so to each boat. A strong tidal current soon swept the lifeboats astern of the *Giang Bee*. It was during this part of the events that earlier air raid damage was revealed –

damaged lowering ropes on one lifeboat parted as it was being lowered into the sea and it spilled its passengers into the darkness of the ocean. The second lifeboat was lowered into the sea, but it had been holed by bomb splinters and soon began taking water and sank.

One survivor recalled the screams for help, mostly women's voices, and the sound of little children calling out for their mothers that came from the damaged lifeboats and those struggling in the sea. Two further lifeboats were successfully launched holding about a hundred people.

At this point one of the destroyers signalled for HMS *Giang Bee* to be abandoned as it was about to be shelled, and many still on board jumped into the sea. At 11.30 pm, six shells struck the *Giang Bee*, and terrified figures could be seen jumping from the deck, soon ablaze from end to end. Glowing red, the ship sank within minutes. The destroyers then sailed away, leaving several hundred women, children and men struggling and drowning in the sea.

Most of the officers and crew died either on board as the ship went down, or drowned after jumping into the darkened sea without a boat or raft. From the 300 people on board there were just over a hundred survivors, and almost all of them

Plymouth Naval Memorial.

ended up in either the men's or women's internment camps at Palembang in Sumatra.

Following the war, a survivor recorded in 1946 that Sub Lieutenant Evans was last seen on board HMS *Giang Bee* at about 7.30 pm on 13 February 1942. He was twenty-seven years old and is commemorated on the Plymouth Naval Memorial, the Liverpool Naval Memorial, and in the Memorial Library at King Edward VI School.

bid its angry tumult cease,
And give, for wild confusion, peace
William Whiting, *Eternal Father, Strong to Save*

Chapter 19

PATRICK GEOFFREY MARSHALL OVERTON

Leading Aircraftsman, Royal Air Force Volunteer Reserve
21 May 1942

Up, up the long, delirious, burning blue
I've topped the wind-swept heights with easy grace
John Gillespie Magee, *High Flight*

During the summer of 1940 when the ever-present threat of German aircraft in the skies over Britain prevented the training of aircrew, the British Government established the Empire Training Scheme. It was a joint military aircrew training programme for the air forces of the United Kingdom, Australia, Canada, New Zealand and Southern Rhodesia. Known variously as 'The Plan' or 'The Scheme', it was responsible for approximately half the pilots, navigators, bomb aimers, air gunners, wireless operators and flight engineers receiving their training.

Although the United States was still a neutral country, and there was a strong national desire to keep out of any European war, the American Government appreciated that German aggression presented a real threat with serious international implications. Accordingly, negotiations to establish training facilities as part of the Empire Training Scheme were successful, and in 1941 a three-phase flying training programme was set up, operated by the United States Army Air Corps and based in the Southeast Air Corps Training Centre (SEACTC). Called 'The Arnold Scheme', it was named after General H.H. 'Hap' Arnold, who instigated the scheme with the full co-operation of President Roosevelt.

Training took place in separate primary, basic and advanced flying schools within the SEACTC area, which included the states of Georgia, Alabama, South Carolina and Florida. Each training centre headquarters was assigned a Royal Air Force administrative officer, and each school had an RAF officer who was in charge of discipline and pay. Primary flying courses were undertaken over nine to ten weeks (sixty hours) at civilian contract schools and they were all run by

The Arnold Scheme.

experienced American civilian instructors. The courses were located at Camden in South Carolina, Albany and Americus in Georgia, at both Arcadia and Lakeland in Florida, and Tuscaloosa in Alabama, and run by the United States Army Air Corps (USAAC) and RAF flight instructors. Three types of plane were used: the Vultee BT-13 was a low-wing monoplane; the Harvard At-6; and a biplane, the Stearman Model 75.

Patrick Overton, who arrived at King Edward VI School in September 1929, left to begin farming in July 1935. Later joining the Metropolitan Police in London, he enlisted in the Royal Air Force Volunteer Reserve in early 1940 and was sent to the Aircrews Selection Centre (ASC) in St John's Wood, and because of its central position in the rail transport system (near Marylebone and Euston Stations), the ASC requisitioned Lord's Cricket Ground. Kitted out, they were accommodated in requisitioned blocks of flats – known as RAF Regent's Park – and then marched to the canteen at London Zoo. During a basic three-week training period they received instructions on service life, underwent a rigorous medical and a series of tests in order to weed out unsuitable candidates and to identify the most suitable aircrew from those remaining. Selected for training as a pilot, Patrick was sent as part of the Arnold Scheme to Alabama. A constant stream of relatively fast unescorted passenger ships crossed the Atlantic. They kept a good safety record, which was made possible by naval intelligence, obtained from the ultra secret Enigma code-breaking carried out at Bletchley Park, based near what is now Milton Keynes.

America in 1942 was very different to Britain. Although prices on almost all everyday goods had been frozen, there was no rationing (this began in 1943) and no blackout. Food and fresh fruit were plentiful – all the steaks, eggs and ice cream they could eat, in such contrast to the meagre rations that people in Britain had to live on at the time. There were no restrictions on travel, and the skies were clear and safe. Although the trainees had to get used to a climate that was hot and humid, they were issued with tropical kit to replace the heavy RAF uniforms.

Stearman.

With increased self-confidence and developing new skills, Patrick enjoyed his flying. He was introduced to blind or cloud flying, where a hood was pulled over the cockpit and he flew entirely on instruments, with a pilot in the back seat to keep a look-out. A fellow trainee pilot remembered 'the sheer freedom in the air, away from the threat of interference from enemy aircraft really made all the objectives of the Arnold Scheme come alive,' and it was a special day when those training received the coveted silver wings.

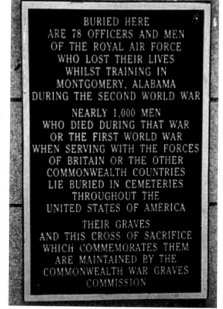

Sadly, a number of trainee pilots were killed, and several in the Vultee BT-13 (known by pilots as 'Valiant') – a basic trainer with a powerful engine, it required the student pilot to operate landing flaps and a two-position variable pitch propeller. An unforgiving aircraft to fly, it had a tendency to shake violently as it approached stall speed, and to

USA memorial.

ground-loop on landing, which caused the plane to cartwheel. This is what happened as Patrick was landing at Arcadia in Florida, and he was killed.

Like seventy-seven other young trainees of the Arnold Scheme, he was buried in the beautiful old Southern Oakwood cemetery annexe off Upper Wetumpka Road in Montgomery, Alabama. A former instructor speaking of all those lost young men: 'He crossed the river to rest in the shade of the trees.'

Patrick Overton is commemorated on the Wellesbourne War Memorial and in the Memorial Library at King Edward VI School.

> *I've chased the shouting wind along, and flung*
> *My eager craft through footless halls of air...*
> John Gillespie Magee, *High Flight*

Notes

1. The country singer Hank Williams is also buried in the Montgomery (Oakwood) Cemetery.

Chapter 20

TERENCE WONG JOY

Sergeant, Observer, 23 Operational Training Unit
26 June 1942

*What of the aircrew, the fliers ... In those young men we may
discern the many faces of courage, the constitution of heroes;
in lonely cockpits at dizzy altitudes, quartering the treacherous
and limitless sea.*

John Terraine, *A Time for Courage*

Although the Germans had turned mainland Europe into a fortress, they could not provide it with a protective roof. In the first two years of the war, the estimated losses of RAF Bomber Command were significantly high. Military historians accept that the casualty figure would have been infinitely greater and the war would have lasted much longer had it not been for the 'scorched earth' policy of Air Marshal Arthur Harris. He possessed something of the earthy, swaggering ruthlessness of an Elizabethan buccaneer. 'There are a lot of people who say that bombing cannot win the war,' he declared in a newsreel interview a few weeks after taking over at Bomber Command. 'My reply to that is that it has never been tried yet. We shall see.'

Since the war he has become a very divisive figure, regarded highly by some, vilified by others. His crews called him 'Butch' (because of his seemingly disregard for the staggering loss of aircrew), and he had become an early convert to strategic bombing, spending the years between the wars working on improving bomb aiming and target marking. Hastings observed that 'from the beginning of the war, he was convinced that given the vast shortcomings of Britain's armed forces compared with Germany, a bomber offensive was inevitable.' Harris had a simple philosophy: carry the battle to the enemy. Destroy their cities as they would destroy ours. Destroy their homes before they destroy ours. Then go back and do it again. He was single-minded in believing that there were no short cuts to defeating Germany from the air. It was necessary, wrote Hastings, to concentrate all available forces for the progressive, systematic destruction of the urban areas of Germany, 'city block by city block, factory by factory, until the enemy became a nation of troglodytes, scratching in the ruins.' He seemed driven, in the words of the historian Anthony Verrier in *The Bomber Offensive*, by an 'elemental tenacity of purpose'.

He wasted no time in giving Germany a sample of what lay in store for them by hitting strong points in the Ruhr, including Essen, with 300 bombers. On 30 May 1942 he startled the German high command by sending 1,000 bombers against Cologne. More than 260 factories were destroyed, water supplies and other facilities were disrupted, more than 300 acres of the city centre were in ruins, 45,000 residents were made homeless and as many as 6,000 were killed. The attack, a turning point in the war, placed Britain in a strong offensive position, whilst Germany took a defensive role.

Terence Joy.

One of the 6,000 aircrew from fifty-three airfields taking part was Sergeant Terence Wong Joy, an observer on a Wellington Mk I of the 23 OTU located at RAF Bourn in Cambridgeshire. Based at RAF Pershore in Worcestershire, 23 OTU was relocated on 29 May 1942 so that it could participate in the Thousand Bomber raid.

Observation and navigation in the air war was a life-or-death science, and many crews lost their way either over the sea, in bad weather, or simply by bad judgement. Air crews, confronted with the statistical probability of their own extinction, soon discovered that early romantic illusions faded as they learned to anticipate their destiny. A bomber pilot remembered: 'You were resigned to dying every night.'

Due to the nature of Terence's father's work, the Wong Joy family were very itinerant, and Terence attended a number of schools – including Blockley Boys' School, Winchcombe Church School, Cheltenham Grammar, Churcher's College in Petersfield and Nelson House in Bristol – before arriving at King Edward VI School in February 1936. He was living with his grandmother in Shipston-on-Stour, and when his father died in 1938, Terence's mother joined him in Shipston. Travelling on the Stratford Blue bus each day, he became firm friends with a fellow pupil, Philip Lomas, who lived in Tredington, who also joined the OTU and was killed in April 1944.

Terence worked at the ironmongers H.F. Sale and Sons, in Sheep Street in Shipston when he left school, and following the outbreak of war he joined the Royal Air Force Volunteer Reserve. As part of 91 Group he joined 23 OTU at RAF Pershore; this was near the village of Bishampton, where his mother, who had recently re-married, now lived.

He had bought a guitar when he lived in Shipston-on-Stour and would sit on the roof of the shop that belonged to his cousin in the High Street, next to the George Hotel, teaching himself. Once in the RAF he joined a dance band and enjoyed playing many of the songs that were so popular in those years – *Indian Summer*, *We'll Meet Again* and *If I Had My Way*.

On the night of 1 June, as 23 OTU supplied fourteen Wellingtons, Terence took part in the second Thousand Bomber raid, this time on Essen. It was less successful than the raid on Cologne, primarily due to haze and low cloud preventing the bombers from finding their targets.

During the next weeks in June, Terence participated in operations against Oberhausen, and on minelaying off St Nazaire, Lorient and Verdon, as preparations began to reassemble the Thousand Force for a raid on Bremen on the wide river Weser for the night of 25 June. Known as Operation *Millennium II*, every type of aircraft available in Bomber Command, and some other commands, was assembled. The actual number varies according to the source, one placing it as high as 1,067, another 'not quite 1,000'. The force was allocated specific targets: the Focke-Wulf ('the sea vulture') factory, the A.G. Weser shipyard, the Deschimag shipyard, and the city of Essen and docks. In his book *Shipston Remembers*, Mike Wells wrote that in just over an hour the raid completely flattened the assembly building of the Focke-Wulf factory and seriously damaged another six buildings on the site. Four other industrial targets were also hit and nearby, 20 acres of the

RAF dance band – Joy on guitar.

Terence with fellow navigators, all of whom were killed during the war.

city centre were badly damaged. The German population, with its natural powers of endurance, stimulated by fear of the Gestapo, were tougher than Bomber Command imagined. The expected demoralization did not occur.

The heaviest loss of aircraft was suffered by 91 Group, losing twenty-three of their 1988 Whitleys and Wellington Mk Is, including Wellington Mk1 X9875, with its crew, Sergeant David Lord, Sergeant Terence Wong Joy, Sergeant Richard Sudbury, Sergeant Colin Cockayne and Sergeant David Rooney. The Wellington crashed into the sea off the Dutch coast. The *Evesham Journal* reported that Terence was missing, and it was only later that his body, with that of Richard Sudbury, was recovered from the sea at Kornwerderzand, south of Harlinge, and buried in Harlingen General Cemetery in Friesland, 24 miles west of Leeuwaden in the Netherlands. Terence and Richard were buried in adjoining graves. The three other crew members were never found and are commemorated on the Runnymede Memorial. Terence Wong Joy is commemorated on the Shipston-on-Stour War Memorial and in the Memorial Library at King Edward VI School.

> *With broken wing they limped across the sky,*
> *Caught in late sunlight.*
> John Bayliss, *Reported Missing*

Chapter 21

ROBERT GRANVILLE PARKS-SMITH

Lieutenant Colonel, Royal Marines
20 August 1942

for a few hours on a hot August morning
Ken Ford, *Dieppe*

On 12 August 1947, *The London Gazette* published a dispatch submitted on 30 August 1942 by Captain J. Hughes-Hallet, Naval Force Commander, to the Commander-in-Chief, Portsmouth. The dispatch reported on the 'proceedings for Operation *Jubilee,* which was carried out on the 18/19 August 1942', attempting to present in positive terms what was in reality an ill-conceived disaster.

'Operation *Jubilee* differed fundamentally from any other Combined Operation that has been carried out by this country in modern times, in as much as it amounted to a direct daylight assault upon an important objective strongly held by the first army of Europe. From the point of view of its perspective in the war as a whole, it may perhaps be compared to the British offensive on the Western Front during 1915. Although from purely a military point of view the results achieved were disappointing, and the heavy casualties sustained regrettable, it is considered that the operation was well worthwhile provided its lessons are carefully applied when the time comes to re-enter France on a large scale.'

In 1942, the outlook for the Allied powers was very far from encouraging and the immediate prospects were bleak. The Afrika Korps were containing British and Commonwealth forces, the Japanese were occupying substantial areas of the British Empire, a Russian military collapse remained a considered possibility, and in the Pacific the forces of the United States were continuing to attempt to halt the advance of the Japanese Navy.

The Russian leader Stalin repeatedly called for an offensive in the west in order to relieve the pressure on his armies, and there were rallies in both London and New York during April 1942 calling for 'a second front now'. An army had been gathered in Britain since 1940, but had no one to fight and nothing to do except train. There was therefore considerable pressure placed on the British Chiefs of Staff to devise and develop an offensive somewhere on the Western Front that would achieve one of two objectives: either draw German divisions from the Russian Front or hold existing divisions in France and therefore prevent additional forces being transferred to the Eastern Front.

A raid against St Nazaire on the west coast of France in March 1942 was a great success. Although hazardous it was carried out with great skill and determination. An old American destroyer was loaded with explosives and rammed the dry dock that was used to repair heavy ships, making it useless to the Germans for the rest of the war.

A similar plan was conceived the following month by Combined Operations Headquarters, to launch a raid on the German-held port of Dieppe on the Channel coast, and during the duration of two tides to inflict a significant amount of destruction to enemy defences and facilities before withdrawing. Parachute units were to attack German artillery batteries on the headlands on either side of a commando assault from the sea, 'a reconnaissance in force,' in Churchill's words, 'to test the enemy defences.'

The parachute operation was cancelled, and when the BBC began broadcasting warnings to the occupied French to evacuate coastal districts, plus warnings from French double agents that the British were showing great interest in the area coupled with a heavy concentration of landing craft in the southern British coastal ports, the German forces at Dieppe were placed on high alert.

Following an unsuccessful exercise and four postponements, Operation *Jubilee* commenced on the warm, moonless evening of 18 August. Although radar stations in England twice warned of 'unidentified vessels', they were ignored, so when Landing Craft Personnel (LCP) ran into five German ships – including armed trawlers – and several of the LCPs were sunk, the element of surprise was lost.

Amongst the force of Royal Marine A Commando was Lieutenant Colonel Robert Granville Parks-Smith. Aged thirty-three, he had attended King Edward VI School between 1917 and 1920 before boarding at Christ's Hospital School in West Sussex, where he was a useful bowler and middle order batsman in the 1st XI during the seasons of 1926 and 1927.

Joining the Royal Marines when he left school, he rose steadily in the ranks and by 1940 was in command of the shore establishment of the Royal Naval Reserve at HMS President. Moored at King's Reach, downstream from Tower Bridge and overlooking the entrance to St Katharine's Dock, it was used for training for defensively equipped merchant ships, gunners and sailors.

The Germans had established very good defences at Dieppe, fortifying the harbour, many of the commanding buildings in the town, and a battery of heavy guns on high ground on each side of the entrance. The seafront was approximately a mile long, with a shingle beach backed by a low sea wall mostly rising no more than 5 feet above the pebbles. Behind the sea wall, and stretching inland for about 220 yards, was an open esplanade of parks and gardens. At the right of the beach, underneath the high western headland, was the town's casino, which had been fortified with two pillboxes facing the sea. The two headlands at either side of the beach were known to be heavily fortified – machine-gun posts and light weapons all sited to command the shore had been skilfully built into caves and were almost invisible from the sea. At the top of the beach was a double row of wire, one on the shingle and one, 6½ feet thick, on top of the sea wall. All the roads leading from the promenade into the town were blocked by 7-foot high concrete walls, 5 feet thick and surmounted by barbed wire, which were further fortified with machine guns. Regrettably, the Allied planners had no clear idea of the strength of these fortifications.

The official report described that: 'The landing was successfully carried out at 7.04 am, shielded by smoke until the last moment. The enemy's fire, however, had not been subdued and the troops met the full force of it immediately on landing.' The Canadian troops of Queen's Own Cameron Highlanders of Canada and South Saskatchewan were virtually all cut down on the beaches. Communications broke down between the troops and the headquarters ship because the Beach Signals Section had been landed with the first assault troops and soon became casualties, with their wireless sets damaged beyond repair. At 8.30 am, the Royal Marines – which included Parks-Smith – were ordered to attack the eastern headland. Parks-Smith was the officer in charge of the Royal Marine Provost party on board a

The harbour front at Dieppe.

Landing Craft Tank (LCT) responsible for the discipline and order over all personnel on the landing on White Beach. He was the oldest serving officer at Combined Operation Headquarters – and had been described by Lord Mountbatten as 'the one really live wire at the time I joined Combined Ops' – and should not have left his duties in London, instead of insisting in going along on the raid. It was his job to be visible and encourage the troops in their efforts – a bit of a sitting duck similar to a second lieutenant in the trenches during the First World War. In his book *Dieppe at Dawn*, R.W. Thompson wrote that when the Royal Marines emerged from the smokescreen laid by aircraft and destroyer, they met the most murderous concentration of fire that had burst upon that dreadful morning. They held on, in the words of the official report, 'with a courage terrible to see'. During the chaos and the slaughter, their commanding officer, Picton-Phillips, ordered the men to abandon the landings. With all beaches out of control, the Canadian commander accepted that the attack was failing and that the objectives of the attack would not be achieved. At 10.45 am, landing craft started to arrive to begin the task of taking men off the beaches. Parks-Smith, who was severely wounded, was assisted to the starboard side to give him greater protection from the shellfire. Sergeant Thomas Badlan managed to steer the shattered LCT clear of the beach and out into the bay. Although a good number were saved, many men were left to die or face captivity.

The defeat and great loss of life sent a shock through the establishment in England, and people quickly began to distance themselves from the responsibility for the failure. Churchill thought that the plan had been ill-conceived and was puzzled by Allied tactics, as indeed were the Germans, who found it incomprehensible that the Canadians were ordered to attack head-on against a German infantry regiment supported by artillery. Simply put, it was a disaster.

Robert Parks-Smith died of his wounds on 20 August 1942 and was buried in South Newington (St Peter Ad Vincula) Churchyard in Oxfordshire. He is commemorated on the Roll of Honour in the Memorial Hall of St John's, Hook Heath, and in the Memorial Library at King Edward VI School.

> *it was a killing ground on a scale that leaves one numb.*
> Ken Ford, *Dieppe*

Notes

1. Canadian Major General Roberts, perhaps unfairly, became the official scapegoat for the failure of the Dieppe Raid and for the loss of Canadian lives. On the eve of the raid, in an attempt to raise the morale of his officers, he said: 'Don't worry men, it'll be a piece of cake!' Afterwards, year after year on 19 August, a small box arrived in the mail for him containing a small piece of stale cake.
2. Sergeant, later Captain, Thomas Badlan was awarded the Distinguished Service Medal for his action on the LCT.

Chapter 22

HERBERT RAY TAYLOR

Captain, 70th (Young Soldiers) Battalion,
Royal Warwickshire Regiment
4 September 1942

The woods that look like clustered weeds,
The chessboard fields, the pin-point spires,
Sun on familiar windows, even
Faint smoke of autumn garden-fires.
Edward Shanks, *The Fighter Pilot Speaks*

At dawn on Friday, 10 May 1940, troop-carrying gliders descended silently beside the crossings of the lower Meuse in south-eastern Holland, and landed on the roof of the key Belgian fort of Eben-Emael with a small elite force of seventy-eight German paratroopers (Fallschirmjäger). Simultaneously, Fallschirmjäger landed around Rotterdam and The Hague, which gave the impression that this was the area of the German main thrust. The subsequent move of French and British forces to meet the offensive coincided with the principal German spearhead through the Ardennes that initiated the decisive *sichelschmidt* (the sweep of the scythe).

On 22 June, following the success of the Fallschirmjäger, Winston Churchill called for the establishment of a corps of parachute troops, and almost immediately volunteers began training at RAF Ringway, outside Manchester. By the end of August, the 1st Parachute Brigade was formed under the command of Brigadier Richard Gale. An Old Boy of King Edward VI School, Gale was awarded the Military Cross during the First World War, and was a contemporary at school of Rex Warneford, who was awarded the Victoria Cross for shooting down a Zeppelin in 1915.

Based at Hardwick Hall, an Elizabethan house in Derbyshire, there was a parachute jump tower, assault courses and a tethered barrage balloon. Although very costly with the loss of thousands of Germany's finest troops, the airborne invasion of Crete in May 1941 reinforced the urgency of an operation by a British parachute battalion. This was successfully achieved when the 1st Airborne

Richard Gale with Field-Marshal Montgomery, Normandy, June 1944.

Division seized a radar installation near Saint Bruneval in France in February 1942.

The aeroplane used was the Armstrong Whitworth Whitley, described by journalist and historian Max Hastings as looking 'for all the world like a rather pedantic middle-aged pipe smoker, with its jutting chin mounting a single .303-inch K Vickers machine gun'. *Flight* magazine wrote that the Whitley 'is as kind to its crew as it is likely to be unkind to any enemy down below,' and possessed a mass of inadequate ancillary equipment that was prone to technical failure – a serious weakness that was to have tragic consequences for the subject of this chapter.

As part of the Airborne Division, 269 Squadron was designated the Glider Pilot Exercise Unit and based at RAF Hurn in Dorset. They used Whitleys employed as glider-tugs and also some that had an exit hatch installed in the fuselage floor to the rear of the aircraft, from where the trainees could bail out.

Ray Taylor (he was known by his second name) was a captain in the 70th (Young Soldiers) Battalion of the Royal Warwickshire Regiment, who in August 1942 responded to the call for volunteers for airborne training and was transferred to RAF Hurn.

Ray's home was in Nuneaton in Warwickshire. He was a boarder at King Edward VI School between 1925 and 1932 and became Captain of Jolyffe House (based on the Warwick Road), played for the 1st XV, gained his 2nd IV colours, and as a member of the Shakespeare Society appeared as Adam in the 1931 production of scenes from *As You Like It* – an evening of entertainment that also included his friend Eric Evans playing Fluellen in *Henry V*.

Leaving school he was articled to a solicitor in Bournemouth, with Eaton and Cockers of St Stephen's Chambers. He moved back to Nuneaton, joined a firm of solicitors, married, enlisted in the Royal Warwickshire Regiment in 1940 and was posted to the Young Soldiers Battalion.

The 70th Battalion, all young volunteers, began in the half-built, empty and dank buildings of a housing estate called Pheasey Farm Estate at Great Barr, Birmingham. Within two months

Ray Taylor.

there were 500 volunteers. The surplus that could not be accommodated were sent to Budbrooke in Warwick, and by May had moved to Malvern in Worcestershire. Later in 1941 they were ordered to Llantwit Major, where their role was to defend the shoreline between Barry and Porthcawl (an area between Swansea and Cardiff), and to erect barbed wire obstacles.

When the Airborne Division began to trawl through the armed services for volunteers to transfer to the newly formed Parachute Regiment, now a captain, Ray Taylor applied.

Initially using Tiger Moths as trainers, these were soon supplemented with Whitleys, and Hart and Hector biplanes were used to tow Hotspur training gliders. The Glider Pilot Exercise Unit, which had been formed from 296 Squadron, provided refresher flying for qualified pilots.

It was during a training flight on board Whitley BD543 on Friday, 4 September 1942 that two observers from their respective 70th (Young Soldiers) Battalion, Second Lieutenant Arthur Twelvetrees (Hampshire Regiment) and Captain Ray Taylor, along with the five-man crew, were killed when the Whitley's port engine failed in the air, and as the pilot, Captain John Callahan, was making an attempt to regain ability to land on the runway, the aircraft stalled to the left and crashed. The flight is recorded as having been an automatic pilot test.

Ray was buried in the Nuneaton (Attleborough) Cemetery. He is commemorated on the Nuneaton War Memorial and in the Memorial Library at King Edward VI in Stratford-upon-Avon. He became the twenty-second casualty from school, some remaining 'missing in action', that was recorded by Denis Dyson, his old Physics master, who maintained a regular correspondence with the Old Boys on active service.

The fall of evening finds us strong,
And kind words bring to us their rich completeness.
A.J.P. Herbert, *The Secret Battle*

Notes
1. There is still mystery surrounding the purpose of this flight and for the presence of both Twelvetrees and Taylor.
2. DFS – Deutsche Forschungsanstalt für Segelflug (General Research Institute for Sailplane Flight).
3. The General Aircraft Hotspur was a training glider, with two crew and carrying eight troops.

Chapter 23

PHILIP SNOWDEN ALEXANDER HILLIER DFC

Flight Lieutenant, Pilot, 6 Squadron
6 September 1942

*There are many dead in the brutish desert, who lie uneasy
among the scrub in the landscape of half-wit stunted ill-will.*
Hamish Henderson, *Elegies for the Dead*

After the German victory in Poland in 1939, the Italian leader Mussolini repeatedly changed his mind whether or not he would enter the war. Although in an alliance with Germany that he had signed in 1939, known as the 'Pact of Steel', Italy remained on good terms with Britain. Nevertheless, the British commander in Africa, General Wavell, believed that Mussolini's pride would eventually drive him to enter the war, comparing his situation to someone at the top of a diving board: 'I think he must do something. If he cannot make a graceful dive, he will at least have to jump in somehow; he can hardly put on his dressing-gown and walk down the stairs again.'

Italy had one of the largest armies – on paper. However, this was far from the reality, because the Italian Regular Army could put only 200,000 troops into action in 1940, and the majority were lightly-armed infantry who were without sufficient motorized transport.

Following the German invasion of France with the French Government leaving Paris and declaring it an open city, Mussolini, clearly a political opportunist, believed that the conflict would end quickly. Although fully aware of Italy's military and material deficiencies, he declared war on Britain and France, with an immediate aim of taking land from British and French colonies in North Africa.

Almost from the outset the Italian's adventure did not go well. Although the forces were not properly equipped and he was advised that such an attack could not possibly succeed, Mussolini ordered an immediate attack into Egypt. On 13 September, the Italians advanced as far as Sidi Barrani, stopped and dug themselves into a series of fortified camps.

Greatly outnumbered, the British forces nevertheless attacked in December, cut off the Italians, reached El Agheila in Libya and captured tens of thousands of prisoners, nearly destroying the Italian Army in North Africa. This caused Hitler to reconsider plans that the German Army High Command had prepared to destroy British influence in the Mediterranean theatre of operations. In view of the situation in Libya, Hitler gave orders for German forces to be sent under the command of Field Marshal Erwin Rommel, and to conduct an 'offensive defence'.

Philip Hillier DFC.

Instead he began offensive operations, and the speed of the German assault was quite breathtaking, with most of the land that the British had captured from the Italians retaken. Tobruk held out and was subjected to a long and intensive siege by the Afrika Korps. Engaged in the defence of the port was Flight Lieutenant Philip Hillier, a member of 6 Squadron of the Royal Air Force Volunteer Reserve, which harried and bombed the German positions at every opportunity. The squadron also maintained attacks against ports and bases on the Italian mainland.

Neither able to take Tobruk or raise the siege, there was a lull in action by both sides until the end of 1941, as they raced to build up their respective strengths. When hostilities resumed in 1942, the Germans took Tobruk and looked as if they were on the verge of sweeping the British Army completely out of Egypt.

During this time, Hillier had moved to a new base at the airfield at Sidi Haneish, 35 miles south-east of Marsa Matruh. Flying a Hawker Hurricane Mk IId, known as 'tank busters', they earned the name 'The Flying Can Opener', attacking ground targets on the Shandur Ranges, and scattering the camels amongst the sand dunes. As a result of two successful sorties against a column of German armoured vehicles near Sidi Rezegh, he was awarded the Distinguished Flying Cross. During one sortie, on 18 June, while attacking a column of armour at extremely low level, Philip's Hurricane struck a tank and lost the tail wheel and part of the rudder. He became the first 'anti-tank ace', with at least nine destroyed. (The award was later announced in *The London Gazette* of 12 November 1942.)

The aircraft took heavy casualties during these sorties from intensive ground fire. During one of these attacks, an anti-aircraft shell exploded in the cockpit of his Hurricane, wrecking the instruments and severely wounding Philip, who nevertheless managed to land his plane at the base at Sidi Haneish.

During his time recuperating from flying, he wrote what was his final letter to his parents. 'Because,' wrote *The Stratford-upon-Avon Herald*, 'it will undoubtedly be a source of comfort to those who, in these tragic days, have also lost near and dear ones,' they published the letter in full, declaring it to be 'redolent of the spirit that permeates the few to whom so much is owed by so many.'

I expect you are worrying about me now that Jerry is starting his tricks again. We in the RAF are having a terrific time. Jerry must be a nervous wreck by now. No human being could stand the way we have been treating him. We think that at this moment we have saved Egypt.

What the future will be I don't know, but the saving of Egypt is worth hundreds such as I. So far I have been lucky and others have not, and I may go on being lucky and you will not have another heart-break, but if I do go the way of those other gallant fellows I go knowing the job we are doing is infinitely worthwhile.

When this particular campaign is over I am going to endeavour to come home and crack Jerry from another end.

Don't look upon this letter as one of those written by a fellow who knows and feels that the end is coming near. No such vision has appeared to me.

I am writing this in my flight office, and it had to be written as I watched these indomitable fighter boys taking off again and again in front of me with precision and no trace of fear. Never have I met such a wonderful fellow-feeling as when I have called at the pilots' mess.

There is the spirit of Drake and Raleigh once more flooding the world, with its quiet courage and devotion to a cause.

It was with a similar precision and spirit that Philip returned to operational flying, but on Sunday, 6 September, the luck he had written about came to an end when he crashed in the desert. He was twenty-six.

Philip Hillier had lived in Bordon Place in Stratford-upon-Avon when he attended King Edward VI School between September 1927 and Christmas 1931, and when his family moved to Harrow he transferred to the County Grammar School (now Harrow High School). He is commemorated on the Harrow County Grammar War Memorial and in the Memorial Library at King Edward VI School. He lies buried in the Fayid War Cemetery, 8 miles south of Ismalia, a small town on the shore of the Great Bitter Lake in Egypt.

> *And, while with silent lifting mind I've trod*
> *The high untrespassed sanctity of space,*
> *Put out my hand, and touched the face of God.*
> John Gillespie Magee, *High Flight*

Notes
1. Philip's brother, Laurence Hillier, of 235 Squadron, was killed over Norway on 3 November 1941 and is buried at Mollendal Church Cemetery in Bergen.

Chapter 24

DEREK HUGH TARVER

Sergeant, Flight Engineer, 102 Squadron
1 October 1942

the time will come when thou shalt lift thine eyes
to watch a long drawn battle in the skies,
while aged peasants, too amazed for words,
stare at the flying fleets of wondrous birds.
Thomas Gray, *Luma Habitabilis,* 1737

While watching the bombing of the city from a rooftop in London on 29 December 1940, Air Marshal Harris turned to Sir Charles Portal, the Commander-in-Chief of Bomber Command, and paraphrasing from the Old Testament announced: 'They have sown the wind, and they shall reap the whirlwind.'

Initially in the war, bombing had been restricted to the dropping of propaganda leaflets and the bombing of strictly military targets, plus a series of diversionary and nuisance raids. The intensity of the 'Blitz' on British cities during late 1940 and early 1941 led to the determination to 'bomb Germany by day as well as by night in ever-increasing measure.' A Liberal Member of Parliament voiced distinct Cromwellian sentiments when he asserted: 'I believe in slaying in the name of the Lord.'

From this point, the British Air Staff held on to the belief in the efficacy and economy of selective attack on German industrial targets, the most vulnerable of which was believed to be oil. Despite the widespread devastation these raids caused, they failed to achieve their objectives. Defences and essential services were maintained and the morale of the civilian population did not break. In fact, German war production continued to rise.

Alexandra Richie wrote in *Faust's Metropolis* that Berlin was the ideal target for air attack. It was Germany's single largest industrial city, containing dozens of huge armaments factories, from AEG to Siemens, Heinkel, Focke-Wulf, Rheinmetall-Borsig, and dozens of others. They produced everything from planes and tanks to small arms and field artillery. It also housed the gigantic government machine that administered all aspects of the war effort.

The Black Bull Inn, Pocklington.

One of the squadrons that was to participate in ever-increasing measure was 102, based near the quiet town of Pocklington in East Yorkshire. They flew the Halifax Mk II as part of Group 4 Bomber Command. It was a large airfield to the south-west of the town, close to Barmby Moor. The *Pocklington Post* in a 1993 article, 'G George', recalled that Mabel's Bar in the Black Bull inn in Market Place was a popular haunt for dozens of men of the Royal Air Force and women in the Women's Auxiliary Air Force, 'who lived life to the full in their off-duty hours.' Locals often thought that the life of these crews was one long party.

Derek Tarver was posted to the Aircrew Reception Centre in St John's Wood, where meals were arranged at the zoo in Regent's Park, and training was organized at Lord's cricket ground. Posted to No. 2 Air Gunnery School, north of Inverness, he flew for the first time in a single-engine Bolton aircraft. After 'passing out', he was ordered first to RAF Harwell for 'crewing up' and then to the Heavy Bomber Conversion Unit at RAF Topcliffe, near Thirsk in North Yorkshire. There the crew were eager to fly together for the first time. They were a happy group of young men, four Canadians – Flight Sergeant Richard Matthews, Sergeant David Benner, Sergeant Sidney Dunn and Sergeant Roy Peters – and three Englishmen – Derek, Sergeant Thomas Parker and Sergeant George Sadler. They soon familiarized themselves with the aircraft. At just over 71½ feet long and with a wingspan of 104 feet and 2 inches, the Halifax Mk II was one of the front-line, four-engine heavy bombers of the Royal Air Force.

Because it was a large port and an industrial centre, one of the earliest raids by Derek's crew was against Hamburg's shipyards, U-boat pens and the large Hamburg-Harburg area oil refineries. It caused widespread damage, mostly in the housing and semi-commercial districts rather than the docks and industrial areas. Although area bombing continued to fail to meet its objectives, 102 Squadron took part at the beginning of the concerted bombing campaign on Berlin that Harris believed would be 'the blow that broke German resistance'.

'The Big One' was what the bomber crews called Berlin, but because of the destructive raids on Hamburg and the Ruhr, the external face of Berlin was changed. Hitler's 5-mile East-West Axis looked like an arrow pointing bombers straight to the heart of the government quarter, and Berliners erected 2 miles of steel poles covered with netting in order to disguise it. There were attempts to build 'false cities' outside Berlin to disorient pilots. Huge anti-aircraft guns were positioned on prominent buildings and medium flak guns and searchlight batteries were placed in and around Berlin, while three 130-feet high flak towers were built in the parks around the government quarter. The 102 Squadron flew the 600 miles to Berlin, delivering bombs in spite of the ferocity of the wall of flak.

Tarver took part in each of the three historic Thousand Bomber raids in May and June 1942, and in the raid on the Ruhr (called 'Happy Valley' by crews), and further raids on Hamburg, Dusseldorf, Hanover and Lubeck, with its tightly packed buildings laid out in a medieval street pattern.

On 16 September, 360 aircraft took part in one of the most successful attacks on Essen and the vast Krupp works, although over 10 per cent of the bombers were lost.

On Thursday, 1 October, Halifax Mk II W7858, piloted by Richard Matthews, took off from Pocklington at 5.57 pm for a raid on Flensburg. Returning from the raid, W7858 crashed into the North Sea. Some days later the body of Richard Matthews was discovered on the beach near Kiel. Those of the other six crew members were never found. Of the twenty-seven Halifax Mk IIs from 4 Group that took part in the raid, twelve, with their eighty-four crewmen, were lost.

Derek Tarver was a pupil at King Edward VI School between 1934 and 1938, and amongst his friends were Terence Joy and Malcolm Kennard. He was aged nineteen when he died and is commemorated in the Memorial Library at his school, in the Garden of Remembrance in Stratford-upon-Avon, and on the Runnymede Memorial beside the Thames in Surrey.

Dawn with its gradual bugles found them soaring,
And sunset made of earth a kindly toy,
A place of sleep and warmth to eke their joy,
And bring them love's release from their exploring.
A.J.P. Herbert, *The Secret Battle*

Chapter 25

THOMAS SERVINGTON PALMER

Corporal, Warwickshire Yeomanry
2 November 1942

Live and let live
No matter how it ended,
These lose and, under the sky,
Lie befriended.
John Pudney, *Graves: El Alamein*

The National Farmers' Union (NFU) was formed in 1908, and two years later, the National Farmers' Union Mutual Insurance Society was established to provide an inducement for farmers to join the NFU. Many boys educated at King Edward VI School crossed Church Street to work in the offices of the NFU Mutual. One of these was Thomas Palmer, who having been at school since 1920, crossed the street in 1927. He enjoyed a successful life there, playing football at the ground on the Tiddington Road (now the site of the headquarters of the NFU Mutual) and becoming the Deputy Chief Clerk.

Thomas Palmer.

97

Mobilized on Saturday, 2 September 1939, Tom Palmer joined the Warwickshire Yeomanry and was to participate in one of history's monumental and significant battles. Sent to the Middle East in January 1940 for garrison and occupation duties in Syria, the Yeomanry became part of the 6th Cavalry Brigade in the 1st Cavalry Division for operations in Iraq and against forces of Vichy France in Syria. The brigade was nominally independent and later in 1942 was placed under the command of 2nd New Zealand Division. For the Yeomanry, the horse had been replaced by a Morris 15cwt CS8 truck. So now 'man's best friend' for the desert war became his water bottle.

As a mechanized armoured unit for the first time, late on 1 August 1941, the Warwickshire Yeomanry was transferred into the Royal Armoured Corps, and re-designated as 9 Armoured Brigade, moved to North Africa in time for the tumultuous campaigns in the Western Desert.

Since it was not possible to fight in Europe even after the German invasion of Russia in June 1941, the Mediterranean remained the focus for the Western Allies in the struggle against Hitler.

By the Summer of 1942, Africa presented tantalizing possibilities for both the Allied forces and for those of the Axis. For the British, Commonwealth and Allied troops, victory meant revenge for humiliating defeats with even the possibility of a toehold into Europe. For Hitler there was the prize of Egypt, the Suez Canal, and the possibility of linking up with German armies advancing south from the Russian Front.

Mussolini, with ambitions to be a warlord, launched a campaign with incompetent commanders leading unwilling soldiers with inadequate weapons that lacked either skill or resolve and had stuttered to a halt requiring German intervention and assistance. Field Marshal Rommel, who had achieved great successes in the campaign in France in 1940, was ordered with the Afrika Korps to advance and seize Egypt.

Montgomery was facing his moment of decision with the Allied armies, and Churchill cabled them: 'The corn will be ripe for the sickle and you will be the reapers.'

On Friday, 23 October 1942, Allied officers were briefed on the battle plan, codenamed Operation *Lightfoot*, and returned to their units to pass on the information. The location was right, with both armies positioned in the open desert between the sea to the north and the soft sand of the Qattara Depression to the south. The objective of 2 New Zealand Division supported by 9 Armoured Brigade (including Tom Palmer's unit) was Miteiriya Ridge, which was intended to be captured by an infantry assault. It was vitally important that they cleared the final minefield before dawn: a process that was called 'crumbling'.

So, following the completion of the initial bombardment, 4th Field Regiment Royal Artillery in support of 9 Armoured Brigade was under orders to move to

El Alamein minefield.

Miteiriya Ridge with the aim of establishing artillery forward beyond the ridge. Covered by the tanks and their supporting arms they were to secure a gap that the Germans would be unable to close. Wireless 'A' sets were individually 'netted' so that the enemy could not pick up the regimental wavelengths. The 'B' radios, used for inter-tank communications, were set. Guns were given a final check and fuel was topped up. As darkness came, everyone took the chance of a good meal. Once the battle started there would only be 'hard tack biscuits'.

The moon rose as the squadrons moved forward, and by 8.00 pm the whole brigade was drawn up in double line. Ronald Bee in his poem *Before El Alamein* referred to 'Dull, quiet and sand hills and a pallid moon'. The artillery barrage opened up at 9.40 pm with more than 1,000 guns, wheel to wheel, pounding the suspected German batteries. At 10.00 pm the barrage switched to the enemy's forward defensive lines. During this time, the engineers set about the dangerous task of clearing mines to make a path for the tanks. One stationery tank could hold up the tank behind and make them all easy targets for the German 88mm gun (designed for use in an anti-tank and anti-aircraft role), 'to be picked off like targets in a fairground,' wrote Peter Rhodes in *For a Shilling a Day.*

After four hours, the barrage was lifted and the tanks with their supporting arms moved forward through the German minefields, with the armoured divisions breaking through the last defence. Casualties on both sides were high, and after a week they were deadlocked. Someone had to smash the anti-tank guns holding up the Allied advance. Montgomery chose the 9 Armoured Brigade, part of the 2nd New Zealand Division comprising the 3rd The King's Own Hussars, the Royal Wiltshire Yeomanry, the Warwickshire Yeomanry, the mechanized 14th Battalion of the Sherwood Forresters, and a New Zealand anti-tank battery to break the enemy and allow Allied forces to stream through into open desert. The desert had been shelled so much that the sand had been reduced to a fine dust. At the pre-battle conference, Montgomery explained to his unit commanders that he was prepared for 100 per cent casualties in order to achieve the objective. General Freyberg said to him: 'The Army Commander will accept 100 per cent tank casualties for success,' and it indeed suffered very nearly that percentage.

On 1 November, Operation *Supercharge* was launched, and the Warwickshire Yeomanry and what was left of 9 Armoured Brigade moved from their positions near Alamein station on an 11-mile approach to the new assault positions. Knowledge of the enemy defences was not known, and the artillery plan was for a bombardment that was three times greater than the attack on 23 October. At 6.15 am on 2 November, with dawn breaking, the tanks moved forward to the first objective and quickly destroyed a battery of Italian guns. The Yeomanry was delayed reaching the start line by unsuspected minefields and pockets of enemy infantry. Fierce tank battles continued throughout the day, and Montgomery decided to exploit his success by striking south. It was during one of the operations, amongst enemy fire with dug-in tanks and machine guns, that Tom Palmer was killed. His body was never found but he is commemorated on the Alamein Memorial that forms the entrance to the El Alamein War Cemetery, west of Alexandria.

With the victory at El Alamein, Churchill ordered the ringing of the church bells in Britain – 'from Land's End to John O'Groats' – which had been silent since the threat of invasion in 1940. The British people had a feeling of redemption and now dared to believe that this was more than just a swing of the pendulum.

A memorial service for those members of the Warwickshire Yeomanry who had been killed during the war was held in St Mary's Collegiate Church in Warwick on 20 December 1944. Thomas is also remembered on the NFU Mutual War Memorial in their head office in Tiddington, on the Wilmcote War Memorial in St Andrew's churchyard, and in the Memorial Library at King Edward VI School.

War memorial at Wooten Wawen.

There are flowers now, they say, at El Alamein;
Yes, flowers in the minefields now.
So those that come to view that vacant scene,
Where death remains and agony has been
Will find the lilies grow –
Flowers, and nothing that we know.
John Jarmain, *El Alamein*

Notes
1. 1st Cavalry Division became 10th Armoured Division. 4th Cavalry Brigade became 9th Armoured Brigade within 10th Armoured Division.

101

Chapter 26

MICHAEL PATRICK WALTON

Lieutenant, Royal Engineers
16 March 1943

I open the casement into his room
So tidy and neat
And the sun shines in and chases the gloom
And the wind blows sweet
May Hill, *The Click of the Garden Gate*

L ife in Stratford-upon-Avon was affected by the war in different ways.
William Dunning, the tailor in Sheep Street, closed for part of each week
owing to 'the calling-up of many of my workers'. To the strict regime of
food rationing and every spare piece of land being turned over to the growing of
food were added restrictions on new furniture. Competitions for the collection of
waste paper were encouraged, as was putting money into a bank because: 'as a
result of enemy action it is unwise to keep large sums of cash about the house
where there is also the possibility of loss by theft, fire and other misfortune.'
Obstructions were placed on any field to prevent the possible landing of a German
aeroplane, road signs were removed, and the 'blackout' restrictions were rigorously
enforced. Many artistic railings were arbitrarily removed, and queues – first for
luxuries and then for essentials – became a social activity. There were shorter
seasons at the Memorial Theatre, the cinema in Greenhill Street offered a
programme of films that changed twice each week, and the dances continued at
the Hippodrome off Wood Street. American servicemen became a familiar sight
in the town, children evacuated from Birmingham attended King Edward VI
School, and masters from the school supported the local campaigns for the Red
Cross and the Spitfire Fund.

By the beginning of 1943, food shortages on the Home Front had become acute.
Of course it had always been important for those in the services to be properly
provided with food, and to support this the British were urged to dig, collect and
sacrifice. When the soldiers tired of the same dull food, however nutritious,
initiative was called for, and flourished even in the Western Desert, where

MICHAEL PATRICK WALTON

Lieutenant Patrick (always known as 'Pat') Walton was with the 12th Company Queen Victoria's Own Madras Sappers and Miners, attached to 12th Company of the 4th Indian Infantry Division. From locals or tribesmen they could buy eggs and tomatoes, or exchange their sweet biscuits for dates, and when supplies could not reach them, the soldiers bartered for milk and cheese.

The Madras Pioneers were formed in 1780 and renamed as Queen Victoria's Own Madras Sappers and Miners in 1911. They served with honour in France and Flanders, and in Egypt and Palestine during the First World War. By 1940 they were commanded by the eccentric and regular church-goer Lieutenant Colonel John Cameron of the Royal Engineers. This explains why Pat Walton, who volunteered in 1940 for the Royal Engineers, was, after receiving his commission, moved to the Indian Army and subsequently posted to the Queen

Michael Walton.

Victoria's Sappers and Miners. By the beginning of 1942, the company arrived in North Africa in time for Rommel's counter-offensive against the Eighth Army.

Only having recently occupied Benghazi, the Eighth Army was ordered to withdraw, and 12th Company and the 4th Indian Infantry Division engineers demolished the port facilities before withdrawing to the east towards the Gazala Line (just west of Tobruk). During the subsequent lull in operations, 4th Indian Infantry Division engineers prepared anti-tank defences and undertook the monumental task of laying half a million mines.

Then, on 27 May, the Germans launched an attack on Gazala, which by 10 June had breached the British defences and forced the Eighth Army to withdraw to the Egyptian border, isolating the garrison at Tobruk.

The 4th Indian Infantry Division was relieved, and with Pat Walton were sent as a defensive unit to Cyprus, where they occupied themselves in anti-invasion exercises on the mountainsides.

The division returned to Egypt in late August and rejoined the Eighth Army in time to pursue the German forces following the battle of Alam el Halfa. Liddell Hart wrote in his book *The Tanks* of 'the thrill and relief of seeing the enemy in retreat, even if only for a short distance – a palpable sign that the tide had turned.'

The 12th Field Company was then assigned to a flying column on 4 November and its mission was to clear minefields where the sand was very soft, and sweep up prisoners, guns and equipment left by the hurriedly retreating Italians.

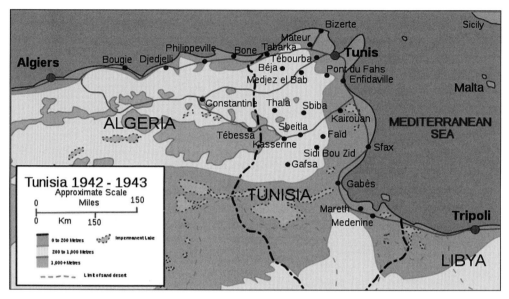

Tunisia.

They were used in a similar capacity at the time of the battle of El Alamein, where their responsibility was to mop up Italian units and salvage equipment. It was not until March 1943 that they rejoined the Eighth Army in an operation capacity in time for the attack on the Mareth Line.

In the meantime, American forces had landed in Tunisia, where they suffered a serious setback at Kasserine Pass, and the German forces now threatened to split the Allied armies. They strengthened the 20-mile Mareth Line that ran across inhospitable desert with a series of hills that provided a natural defence line. It was originally built by the French to defend Southern Tunisia against attacks from the Italians in Libya. Retreating swiftly, the Allies reinforced their position as additional troops and trucks poured in. Their practical experience in desert warfare offered an opportunity to outflank the Mareth Line – what Montgomery called 'a left hook'. By switching his main attack from seaward end to the landward, the forces broke the line and advanced through the inland hills, although heavy rain prevented the use of tanks. During the fierce fighting, Pat Walton was mortally wounded and died on Tuesday, 16 March. He was twenty-one years old.

Pat Walton, who lived at Mount Pleasant Farm off the Alcester Road – where on summer evenings he enjoyed sitting amongst the fruit trees – attended the King Edward VI Preparatory School from May 1929 – Richard Spender was a friend – and joined the Grammar School in 1930, where he later coxed two particularly impressive 1st IV crews in 1933 and 1934. In the autumn of 1934 he moved as a boarder to Ipswich School, where he became a fine rugby player and captained an unbeaten 1st XV during his final year.

He moved to Chester when he finished school and began to study as a quantity surveyor for Messrs Wilson Lovatt, while continuing to enjoy playing rugby, becoming the youngest member of the Chester RFC 1st XV during the 1940-1941 season.

The *Stratford-upon-Avon Herald* reported in April 1943 that the news of his death had been received by his mother and father from Lieutenant David Orchard of the Royal Engineers: 'Pat and I were the best of pals, and I know only too well how very great the loss must be to his dear ones. ... Pat's jemadar wishes me to convey to you the sympathy of all the men in the section, to whom Pat was a splendid officer and friend.'

Pat Walton was buried in the Sfax War Cemetery, south of Tunis, and is commemorated in the Memorial Library at King Edward VI School, and in the Garden of Remembrance in Stratford-upon-Avon.

I hear the click of the garden gate
But it is not he.
May Hill, *The Click of the Garden Gate*

Notes
1. A jemadar either commanded platoons or troops or assisted the British Commander. It was a rank used in the British Indian Army.

Chapter 27

RICHARD WILLIAM OSBORNE SPENDER

Captain, 2nd Battalion, Parachute Regiment
27 March 1943

Of little men, who die that the great Truths shall live.
Richard Spender

On the upper floor of the medieval buildings of the Grammar School in Stratford-upon-Avon is the Council Chamber, where for centuries the Town Council of the Borough held its meetings. In the centre of the room there is a long Jacobean table in dark oak. Deeply carved into it are the names of hundreds of boys who were prefects of King Edward VI School. Not exactly encouraged, it was nevertheless a tradition that lasted more than a hundred years. Amongst the finely carved names there is one that has been carefully and artistically chiselled: a boy who made a deep and lasting impression on the school – Richard William Osborne Spender.

Challenge was the keynote of Richard Spender's life. From an early age he embraced every opportunity, and with infectious enthusiasm worked determinedly to excel in all he did. He had a great appetite and enjoyment for life, and possessed an intense happiness that made him an exciting companion or friend. He filled a room, not with his stature – for he was not tall – but with his energy, and there were few in his home town that were not aware of him. With enormous personal empathy and a great capacity for fun, he had unusual powers of initiative and leadership. His friends saw in him an acutely sensitive, kind and thoughtful spirit. He loved Warwickshire and the Avon, and when war came in 1939 he put his studies to one side and took, as he wrote, 'a sword against the world for truth'.

In September 1927, Richard was enrolled in the King Edward VI Preparatory School, and in January 1930 transferred to the Grammar School, beginning a decade of intense affection for and an enthusiastic involvement in the life of the school.

School for Richard was a serious business, and by the time he reached the Sixth

Form he was the chief or deputy chief of every form of activity. One of his masters recalled that 'somehow he always had to play the lead. It was inevitable. What was strange was that, almost without exception, the other boys agreed.' A contemporary remembered that Richard arrived at school one morning dishevelled and clearly the worse for wear, and staggered up the stairs to the Sixth Form Common Room. Seizing a long wooden bench on which to sleep, he misjudged the position of the long window that was covered with netting against possible bomb blasts. The end of the bench went straight through the window as he settled down to sleep. 'It's just Dickie,' was the response of the headmaster. The same affectionate indulgence would follow him to the Tunisian desert.

Richard Spender.

He grew to love the river Avon and school rowing became indispensible for him, earning his 1st IV colours. He gained his 1st XV colours and became Captain of the School. His powers of persuasion and expression were valuable assets in the Debating and Dramatic Societies, and he also edited the school magazine, *The Stratfordian*, in which his first verses began to appear. Walking the same fields as William

KES Cadet Corps, 1938. Richard Spender, 2nd row, 4th from left.

Shakespeare, Richard had developed a keen understanding of language and literature, and as the years passed his poetry developed a great perception, and his technical mastery matured.

At nineteen years old, Richard Spender gained the Bracegirdle Exhibition in Modern History at St Catherine's College, Oxford, but decided to set it aside and joined the Army as a private in the 70th Young Soldiers' Battalion of the Gloucestershire Regiment. He applied for a commission, joined the 163 Officer Cadet Training Unit at Pwllheli, and on completion was posted to the London Irish, becoming the proud wearer of the green caubeen with the pale blue hackle. It was perhaps the most fantastic and the most theatrical of all British military headgear, and Richard continued to wear it to his last day, even when a paratrooper in North Africa.

Towards the end of 1941, he was given the rank of temporary captain and became an Instructor in the Original Experimental Battle School at Barnard Castle. Instructing others to deal with dangers that he had not faced himself made Richard Spender deeply dissatisfied. In spite of the hard work and the risks at the Battle School, he was not involved in the real war, and although it is difficult to assign human actions to any one source, it was perhaps this dissatisfaction that led him to volunteer in the summer of 1942 for the Parachute Regiment.

The commander of the Parachute forces was General Richard 'Windy' Gale. Like Spender, he was an Old Boy of King Edward VI School in Stratford-upon-Avon. Arriving at Bulford, Richard walked into the office and announced: 'I'm a new Parachutist. What do we do?' The officer present, Victor Dover, had only joined the regiment that day himself, and their subsequent conversation established an enduring friendship. The commanding officer at Bulford was the inspirational Colonel John Frost, and he called the two new recruits 'Dickie 1' (Spender) and 'Dickie 2' (Dover).

In late Autumn, 2nd Battalion, Parachute Regiment were told that it would form part of the Expeditionary Force to be sent to North Africa. Richard's poetry was beginning to appear in national newspapers and journals, and the columnist 'Peterborough' writing in *The Daily Telegraph* spoke of a comparison between Richard's work and that of Rupert Brooke. During the voyage to North Africa, a collection of his poems, *Laughing Blood*, was published, some of which had already appeared in *The Observer*, *Country Life*, *The New York Times* and *The Times Literary Supplement*.

Arriving in Algiers, he discovered some men from his old battalion in the London Irish Rifles who were happy to see the caubeen in North Africa. He grew a large beard and side whiskers, which like the caubeen he was allowed to keep. His friend Victor Dover re-emphasized that it was again 'something which no one else would have been allowed to do – he had a way with him.' His popularity was immediate and complete.

The fighting became hard and constant and patrolling was regular. During the fighting for Djebel Mansour, Richard was clearly seen standing on an exposed hill waving his blackthorn walking stick and cheering on his men, 'blue plume flashing challenge to the sun and the Hun.' The battalion moved to the area of Mohammed el Kassin, commonly called 'Cork Wood', where for twenty-four hours Richard was in a tree sniping at the enemy with significant success.

During the early part of the Battle of Tamera in March 1943, the Germans launched a number of infantry assaults in an attempt to drive the battalion from their defensive positions. Although all these assaults failed, it was clear that the rate of attrition on 2nd Battalion and the rest of the brigade was unsustainable. They were ordered to withdraw to new positions along a river bed, and as John Frost remembered, 'a salvo of shells poured in among us, but we could at least be thankful for the cover afforded by the banks.' More than half the shells did not explode, and it was here that with his indomitable humour Richard Spender composed his last short poem:

> *Thud*
> *In the Mud,*
> *Thank Gud,*
> *Another dud.*

Following withdrawal to the rear for rest, the battalion was back in action on the night of 27 March. Victor Dover remembered: 'It was a beautiful warm night and the noise of the shells above was orchestral in its infinite variation.' The battalion made good progress, but then C Company, with Richard Spender, began to meet strong opposition, which stiffened quickly as the Germans built into a major counter-attack. In the darkness, closely packed groups of the enemy advanced through the trees, using the slope of a hill to keep momentum. At one point the counter-attack almost enveloped C Company. Leading a charge against a machine-gun position, Richard's voice was clearly heard calling out: 'Come on, my merry men, we're going to attack. Come on, attack! Attack.'

He was found some time later lying where he had fallen. Richard's friends in the battalion, and there were many of them, were deeply saddened by his death. The news was a very hard knock for his old school. A friend, Bill Collins, who had been given his first lessons in coxing a racing boat by Spender, remembers 'a shocking sense of loss throughout the school', and the headmaster, conducting a private memorial service in the Guild Chapel, recalled that 'He knew friendship is the soul of life, and nothing in all his ambitions could make him false to that conviction.'

Victor Dover wrote an engaging and detailed book, *The Silken Canopy*, about his experiences in the Parachute Regiment, where he reached the rank of major, fought at Arnhem, and was awarded the Military Cross. Writing with much affection of his friendship with Richard Spender, he remembered him as an acutely sensitive, kind and thoughtful spirit. 'His death left a gap of friendship which was never filled.' The sentiments expressed by John Buchan about Raymond Asquith – a young man of great popularity and promise who was killed on the Somme in 1916 – serve equally for Richard Spender: 'He loved his youth. And his youth has become eternal. Brilliant and brave, he is now part of the immortal England which knows not age or weariness or defeat.'

Richard is commemorated in Holy Trinity Church and on the KES Boat Club Memorial in the Garden of Remembrance in Old Town, Stratford-upon-Avon and in the Memorial Library at King Edward VI School. One of the four school Houses is named in his memory. His *Collected Poems* were published in 1943 and were reprinted annually until 1964. A new collection of all his poems with a biography is to be published.

Richard Spender was buried in the Tabarka Ras Rajel War Cemetery. It is 93 miles north-west of Tunis and almost on the Algerian border. On the headstone above his grave, his father chose to have Richard's own words inscribed:

As we have lived
So let us die.
In high proud exultation.
Let us repay
Laughing blood with spilt.

Chapter 28

DAVID OVERBURY

Corporal, 46th Reconnaissance Regiment,
46th Infantry Division
2 April 1943

Now strike the flag, the panther green and gold ...
They are not needed, fold them, lay them by.
Reconnaissance Regiment

Some 93 miles north-west of Tunis and almost right on the Algerian border is the Tabarka Ras Rajel War Cemetery. Just 7 miles east of the coastal town and laid out like an English garden, there are 500 Commonwealth graves. Lying 50 feet apart are two friends from King Edward VI School who rowed in the same 1st IV, and who were killed within five days of each other. Richard Spender on 27 March, and David Overbury on 2 April.

David lived in Wellesbourne, near Warwick, and with his brother James joined the school in May 1933. He loved rowing and was awarded his 1st IV cap the same year he won the Brickwood Skulls, in an energetic final against Richard Spender. As a corporal in the Cadet Corps, he took part in 'battles' at Sutton Park near Birmingham and at the annual Public Secondary Schools Cadet Association's camp at Marlborough Common, near the Bronze Age barrow.

Leaving school in December 1939, David joined the Midland Bank in Shipston-on-Stour. Still there as the HSBC Bank, it is a Grade II listed building. Later, in 1940, David enlisted in the Infantry Brigade Reconnaissance Group, which in February 1941 became the Reconnaissance Corps. An elite corps, their orders in battle were to probe ahead and gather vital tactical information for infantry divisions, and also to screen the flanks of main advances.

Initially established at Winchester in February 1941, the corps later moved to Lockerbie in Dumfries. Raised from a number of regular army units, all the men had to take an IQ test plus additional tests. Those who succeeded undertook a five-week course with various technical units to determine respective roles, whether as a driver, a wireless operator or mechanic, although most became proficient in two of them. The chief instructor was Lieutenant Colonel N.R. Blockley. They enjoyed the esteem and great pride of belonging to an elite unit.

Reconnaissance regiments were organized into a headquarters squadron that included anti-tank, signals, and mortar troops, and three reconnaissance ('recce') squadrons. Within the recce squadron were three scout troops and an assault troop. The scout troops were equipped with light reconnaissance cars – the Humber Light Reconnaissance Car – with Bren gun carriers. The assault troop were lorried infantry and used to overcome enemy resistance.

David became a corporal in the 46th Reconnaissance Regiment, Reconnaissance Corps, 46th Infantry Division, which was under the command of First Army. Based at Lyminge, near Folkestone in south-east Kent, they underwent further training at Godalming in Surrey. Following nine days' embarkation leave, during which David returned home to Wellesbourne, the division left the United Kingdom on S/S *Duchess of Bedford* and arrived in Algiers on 17 January 1943, joined 5 Corps on 3 February and carried out 'active patrolling'.

Believing that the battle at Kasserine had led to the Allies reinforcing their southern line in Tunisia at the expense of the north, the Germans launched an attack against Medjez-el-Bab in the west, a second to the north towards Beja, and a third pushing west to Medjez. The attack on Medjez was defeated, while intense fighting in terrible weather halted the move to Beja.

In the north, the German attack across French-held and lightly defended hills between Cap Serrat and Sedjenane progressed, but by 2 March had been halted by costly counter-attacks by elements of 46 Infantry Division.

The German attacks in the centre and south were abandoned, but they were able to occupy high ground around Medjez, when French battalions withdrew, and this created a dangerous salient.

On 28 March, 46 Division was ordered to regain the initiative, and the days that followed saw persistent and fierce fighting. It was during this time that David Overbury was killed. He was twenty-one. The fighting in Tunisia was to continue for only a few more days before the Germans surrendered.

David is commemorated on the Wellesbourne War Memorial, on the KES Boat Club Memorial in the Garden of Remembrance in Old Town, Stratford-upon-Avon, and in the Memorial Library at King Edward VI School.

> *To-day some silent valley of Tunisia*
> *Shall tremble at their stroke from sky unleashed,*
> *And, with the night, perhaps some God looking down*
> *With dull, cold eyes, by the near stars, will see*
> *One lonely, grim battalion cut its way*
> *Through agony and death to fame's high crown*
> Richard Spender

Notes
1. RAF Wellesbourne Mountford was the base for 22 Operational Training Unit, part of 6 Group Bomber Command.

Chapter 29

FRANK GIFFORD ROTHERY

Major, 5th Battalion, Hampshire Regiment
9 April 1943

Winds carve this land
And velvet whorls of sand
Annul footprint and grave
Of lover, fool and knave.
John Pudney, *Landscape: Western Desert*

'A form of romantic haze enveloped the desert war,' wrote Richard Doherty in his history of the Eighth Army, *A Noble Crusade*. 'For those who did not have to fight there, it was a clean war and both sides appeared to behave in a chivalrous fashion.'

The fighting took place in a narrow strip of scrub and sand along the Mediterranean coast, seldom more than 50 miles wide. Between September 1940 and May 1943, the rival armies – affected by their ability to move fuel, ammunition, food and water – were engaged in a series of campaigns that covered more than 2,000 miles. Although there are few instances of anything approaching an atrocity in North Africa, that does not mean that men were not dying and being maimed in circumstances as horrible as any other theatre of the war. There is proof of this in Keith Douglas's description of the body of a dead German gunner in his poem *Elegy for an 88 Gunner*: '*how on his skin the swart flies move; the dust upon the paper eye and the burst stomach like a cave.*' Whatever the reason, this romantic haze, continued Doherty, 'placed the mantle of hero on the shoulders of desert veterans.' This remained the case as the fighting in North Africa was drawing to a close, and when, on 9 April 1943, Major Frank Gifford of 5th Battalion, Hampshire Regiment, was killed.

Frank had been a boarder in School House at King Edward VI School. As an active member of the Cadet Corps it was natural that when he returned home to Weston-super-Mare and the war clouds gathered he should join the Territorial Army. He joined on 1 July 1939 and was commissioned into the Hampshire Regiment based at Aldershot. The regimental diary reports that by November 1940 he was a captain in the 2nd Battalion, and by March 1941 had been promoted to major. There was always extensive training and the regular brigade tournaments in boxing, football and hockey to organize, plus the visit of the Commander-in-Chief Home Front, General Sir Alan Brooke. Then, in September 1942, Frank was transferred to command A Company of 5th Battalion in preparation for action overseas. Orders came at the beginning of the New Year, and on 7 January, as part of the 46th Infantry Division for Operation *Torch*, the Battalion embarked on HMS *Leopoldville* and nine days later landed at Algiers. Frank arrived in North Africa around the same time as the other KES boys Richard Spender and David Overbury. Almost immediately, they sailed on HMS *Royal Ulsterman* to Bone, to the east of Algiers, near the Tunisian border, where they remained until 31 January, when they moved to the Allied Front at Kazar Mezouar (Hunt's Farm). A company of the 5th Battalion was sent 12 miles further ahead to Sidi Nsir, with their headquarters in a small railway station. They were ordered to occupy a craggy hilltop position in order to listen to and monitor German movements, and hold any advance of tanks down the narrow valley below.

Messerschmitt Me 109s began to strafe the valley on the night of 25 February, and with the dawn of the following day, B Company of the 5th Battalion was attacked in overwhelming strength by German paratroopers, elements of 10 Panzer Tiger Division and the 501st Heavy Tank Brigade in Operation *Ox Head*. For the Allies there was great concern that such a powerful battle group would break through their defences. B Company, supported by 155th Battery Royal Artillery, dug in, and from dawn faced an unrelenting German assault that knocked out all their guns and the crews who had stood firing over open sights at the German tanks. Realizing that their position was precarious, the battalion withdrew to a point called 'Hampshire's Farm'. Most of the officers and men had no battle experience, and only nine gunners survived. Their heroic resistance helped delay the Germans for forty-eight hours, thereby allowing for extra mining of the road and the reinforcement of Hunt's Farm.

On 1 March, the Germans attacked again, but the battalion hung onto their remaining position. The following day the Germans withdrew. During the rest of the month, all the battalion took part in defensive patrolling and received five officers and 150 men as replacements. By the end of the month it was the turn of Frank Gifford's A Company of the 5th Battalion to face the German assault.

The final attack on Tunis would have to be mounted and launched from the area of Medjez-el-Bab, just west of Tunis. It was necessary that the Germans were driven out of the commanding positions that they had acquired north and north-east of the town. The 46th Division, plus the Parachute Brigade (which included Captain Richard Spender) attacked towards Sedjenane and drove the Germans back. At the same time, the Mareth Line – the narrow stretch of land that was the gateway to Southern Tunisia – was assaulted successfully by the Eighth Army (which included David Overbury) by a great outflanking movement across the desert that reached 45 miles behind the German lines.

On 5 April, Frank Gifford's A Company was part of a campaign of advance to take Pichon and the Fondouk Gap so that 6th Armoured Division could intercept the retreating Afrika Korps. The battalion arrived in El Ala just before daylight on 7 April, after a two-day journey by truck, followed by a wet march to the assembly area in a cactus grove. The plan was for the 1/4th to capture Pichon and the high ground 1,000 yards to the south-east and then take the high ground above Pichon. When these objectives had been achieved, the 5th were to pass through and secure the northern side of the Fondouk Gap. At dusk the 1/4th and the 2/4th battalions marched silently for 6 miles and then waited until 4.30 am.

Advancing on the village of Pichon in a howling gale that covered everyone and everything with thick dust, the leading companies of A and B, the 1/4th became pinned down by heavy machine-gun fire, mortars and artillery. D Company carried out a left flanking movement, and by noon the village was taken.

Meanwhile, the 5th Battalion, without natural cover, had been forced to lie in the open and came under heavy fire from mortars dropping all around them. A Company was sent in to 'wrinkle the Germans out'. Rothery, with a group of sixty

Medez-el-Bab war cemetery.

men, was ordered to clear some persistent machine-gun fire and managed to secure the side of a hill. Deciding to take a short cut around the hill, they ran into a machine-gun post, and it was here that Frank Rothery was killed. He was thirty-six. Later in the day, the battalion advanced through Pichon with tanks and captured the vital high ground of the Foundouk Gap. A month later, Tunis fell and the campaign in North Africa was over.

Frank Gifford is commemorated on the memorial in the Medez-el-Bab War Cemetery, 60 miles west of Tunis, and on the Hampshire Regiment Memorial in Basingstoke, 19 miles from Winchester. He is also remembered in the Memorial Library at King Edward VI School.

Vor der kaserne vor dem grossen Tor
Stand eine Laterne und steht sienoch devour[1]
Hans Leip

Notes

1. The opening two lines of Lily Marleen, the German love song that became very popular with troops of both sides that were stationed around the Mediterranean and particularly in the Western Desert campaign.

In front of the barracks, In front of the main gate,
Stood a lamppost, If it still stands out front.

Chapter 30

PATRICK ENGLISH

Leading Stoker, Royal Navy, HMS *Beverley*
11 April 1943

If I take the wings of the morning,
And dwell in the uttermost parts of the sea;
Even there shall Thy hand lead me;
And Thy right hand shall hold me.
Psalm 139

After 1941, as the war escalated and widened, the importance of the convoy system as a lifeline for Britain became critical, so the involvement of the Navy in the Atlantic intensified. Winston Churchill was later to write that the Battle of the Atlantic was the dominating factor all through the war, and that the 'only thing that ever frightened me ... was the U-boat peril.' It was from the summer of 1940 and through much of 1941 that the U-boats enjoyed what their crews referred to as 'Die Gluckliche Zeit' (the Happy Time). Working in Wolf Packs with devastating effect, a great number of naval and merchant ships were sunk (including SS *Temple Moat*, with sixteen-year-old Malcolm Kennard).

Such losses forced the British into a fundamental assessment of tactics, leading to the introduction of permanent escort groups, which it was hoped would improve the co-ordination and effectiveness of their ships. These changes were certainly helped by the increased availability of the number of escort ships, as fifty old ex-American destroyers came into service under the Lend-Lease Agreement between Britain and the United States. Although still remaining officially neutral, by 1941 the public opinion in America had begun to swing against Germany, and the agreement was a way the United States of America could help Britain whilst staying out of the hostilities itself. President Roosevelt had declared a policy of 'all aid to Great Britain short of war'.

The USS *Branch* (DD-197) was a Belmont Class destroyer launched in April 1919, and engaged in tactical exercises along the Atlantic coast. Placed out of commission in 1922 and held in reserve until October 1940, she was transferred to the British Navy in the Destroyers for Bases Agreement and renamed HMS *Beverley*.

During the Second World War it became a custom of British towns and groups to raise money for an aircraft or a naval vessel, and HMS *Beverley* was officially 'adopted' by Beverley in Yorkshire, and was 'provided with many comforts'. However, HMS *Beverley* was 'awarded' to the Welsh town of Merthyr Tydfil, which had raised £57,000 during Warship Week. Subsequently, the town was informed that its donation had been used to finance the cost of HMS *Beverley*, and the local newspaper, the *Merthyr Express*, continued to carry stories of the ship's activities. Meanwhile, Beverley continued to support the ship until it was sunk, and in 2003 a memorial of Portland Stone to the men of the ship was dedicated in the Memorial Gardens on Hengate, in Beverley.

Patrick English, the son of a Stratford-upon-Avon bank manager who lived in Rother Street, had been privately educated at The Laurels in Clifford Chambers before attending King Edward VI School from 1922 until December 1926. His brother Marcus was at KES until the family moved to Nantwich, a market town in Cheshire, where the brothers continued their education.

Patrick joined the Royal Navy and was posted as a leading stoker (the colloquial term used to refer to a marine engineering rating) to HMS *Beverley* on the completion of its refit and modifications for trade convoy escort service in October 1940, and was deployed as part of the escort on thirty-one convoys between January 1941 and its final convoy in March 1943. Initially on West African and Malta convoys, she was transferred at the beginning of 1942 as escort to the North Atlantic Approaches, and from April on the treacherous Russian Arctic convoys. The route around Norway was dangerous as it brought the convoy close to German air and submarine forces. It had to avoid the Arctic ice floes, there was frequent fog and the weather was constantly appalling. Ending up in the sea meant instant oblivion.

HMS *Beverley* became a member of the 'support group' to reinforce convoys from Iceland to Murmansk. Unlike regular escort groups, support groups were not directly responsible for the safety of any particular convoy, thereby giving them much more tactical flexibility and allowing them to detach ships in order to hunt submarines that had been spotted by reconnaissance aircraft.

Although it was true that by the end of 1942 a large number of ships were still being sunk, and at a rate greater than could be quickly replaced, the American shipyards had begun to swing into full production. So in spite of the fact that the first months of 1943 were for Britain some of the most disastrous of the war in terms of merchant shipping lost, leading to the supplies of fuel becoming critically low, the climax in the Atlantic was approaching.

Just before Christmas 1942, HMS *Beverley* had arrived into St John's, Newfoundland, with only 5 tons of fuel left in the bunkers, having been through an Atlantic storm considered the worst within memory. Fitted with the new Hedgehog weapon (an anti-submarine mortar), HMS *Beverley* was now considered

HMS Beverley.

'an experienced North Atlantic escort', and early in 1943 doggedly, and successfully, pursued one U-boat that in a 'pack' of forty was causing havoc amongst the merchant ships.

Almost at the start of what became its final convoy, HMS *Beverley*, 'in thick weather', collided with the merchant ship SS *Cairnvalona*, lost her anti-submarine equipment and seriously slowed her passage. Now at the rear of the convoy early in the morning of 11 April, and very vulnerable, it was sighted by U188 about 530 miles south of Greenland. Three torpedoes hit the ship. Those below decks and in the engine room had no chance as HMS *Beverley* sunk within minutes. Only four survived as 151 men, including her commanding officer, went down with the ship.

Telegrams were sent to the families of the crewmen telling them that they were 'missing', and then sometime later when all hope was over, a letter was sent confirming their loss. Patrick English was twenty-nine. He is commemorated on the Portsmouth Naval Monument on Southsea Common, which overlooks the promenade, and in the Memorial Library at King Edward VI School.

What nice easy prey for the Huns
Who trailed them with bombers and U-boats
And sank them with 'tin-fish' and guns.
Edward Carpenter, Merchant Seaman

Chapter 31

WILLIAM JOHN STILES

Sergeant, Air Bomber, 49 Squadron
18 August 1943

Like rare birds the curious migration of the bombers were
Studied and tracked.
Daniel Swift, *Bomber County*

As a war correspondent, Martha Gellhorn witnessed the reality of battle both in its preparation and engagement, and later, in her book *The Face of War*, she wrote of the bomber pilots, 'polite and kind and far away', as they faced another mission. She could have been writing of 49 Squadron and the crew that included Sergeant William Stiles, preparing to fly on a cloudless, moonlit night against a difficult and dangerous target. 'Every man went tight and concentrated into himself, waiting and ready for the job ahead, and the seven of them who were going together made a solid unit, and anyone who had not done what they did and would never go where they were going, could not understand and had no right to intrude.'

Posted from 1654 Heavy Conversion Unit at Wigsley to RAF Fiskerton on 17 June 1943, William Stiles became a member of a crew that for the next two months flew together against German and Italian targets. These included the docks at Krefeld in North Rhine-Westphalia, Friedrichshafen, Spezia, and Gelsen-kirchen – the first attack since 1941 on this oil target in the Ruhr – during which

RAF Fiskerton memorial.

120

they had a near brush with disaster when, in collision with a Ju 88, the Lancaster's port flaps and outer fuel tank were damaged. In late July and August, still in Lancaster JA691, their missions were against Nuremburg, Hamburg and Milan. Following a succession of missions, they return from Milan on the morning of 15 August particularly tired.

The Avro Lancaster was the finest heavy bomber of the Second World War. With its evocative sound in flight and distinctive twin-tail fin and four Rolls-Royce Merlin engines, it carried a crew of seven. The pilot was the commanding officer, irrespective of rank. Primarily a night bomber, the crews were generally in their early twenties. However, the crew of JA691 was one of the exceptions. The flight engineer, Sergeant Leslie Henley, was forty-three; both the navigator, Sergeant Leslie Freeman, and William Stiles were thirty-one; the pilot, Flying Officer Harry Randall, was also in his thirties, and the wireless operator, Reginald Fowlston, was twenty-nine. Only the Australian mid-upper gunner, Sergeant Norman Buchanan, and the rear gunner, Sergeant Robert Slaughter, both in their early twenties, were the average.

At 9.00 am in the morning of Tuesday, 17 August, the order was received at RAF Fiskerton from Bomber Command Headquarters in High Wycombe for an attack that night on the German research establishment at Peenemünde. The operation, codenamed *Hydra*, had been meticulously planned and had three requirements – a full moon, no cloud over the target, and clear weather over England for the bombers' return. The security surrounding the briefing for the operation was very high. One survivor remembered that it was the only briefing he attended when the hut was surrounded by Service police, and crew members had to show their identification. Crews were told that the target was 'a visual radio-location laboratory and aircraft testing site'.

Churchill had instructed: 'We must bomb by moonlight, although the German night fighters will be close at hand.' The importance of a successful raid was emphasized and the crews told, 'If the attack fails, it will be repeated the next night and on ensuing nights regardless, within practicable limits, of casualties.'

The German Rocket programme at Peenemünde was developing 'vengeance weapons', the V1 pilotless 'flying bomb', the V2 Rocket, and a supergun. The order was to destroy the facility, and for precision the aircrews would have to drop bombs during the full moon from 8,000 feet instead of the normal 19,000 feet. Such was the importance of the operation that most of the squadrons were led by their wing commanders, and throughout the attack the master bomber (Group Captain Searby, commanding officer of 83 Squadron) circled above and around the target, calling in Pathfinder markers and directing crews to target the markers.

At 9.46 pm, Lancaster JA691 roared down the runway, with Lincoln Cathedral silhouetted by the setting sun. It crossed the North Sea, over Jutland and Zeeland

The crew of Lancaster JA691. William Stiles, back row, 2nd from right.

and the Baltic, until at the Arkona Peninsula they began their approach run on Peenemünde.

In order to divert the attention of German night fighters, a group of Mosquitoes, imitating Pathfinder markings, undertook an air raid on Berlin. Initially this operation, called *Whitebait*, drew most of the night fighters, as the 560 bombers dropped nearly 1,800 bombs on their main targets over Peenemünde. Realizing their mistake, the German night fighter controllers quickly instructed their fighters to intercept the bombers on their flight home.

The pilot of a Me 110, Oberleutnant Hans Meissner, later recalled: 'It was a bright moonlit night and the sky was cloudless. Flying north I picked up a contact at 3,700-metre altitude, north-east of Aabenraa in Denmark.' It was JA691, and presented an easy target. Approaching the Lancaster low from behind, Meissner opened fire at 50 metres. This was the first night on which the Germans used the new Musik weapon: twin upward-firing cannon fitted in the cockpit and that fired beneath a bomber, where a Lancaster was most vulnerable. It was 3.01 am. JA691 exploded and fell burning to the ground. One witness on the ground described that in the sky he saw what appeared to be fireworks flying through the air.

The seven members of the crew were buried in Aabenraa on Saturday, 21

WILLIAM JOHN STILES

August in a military funeral arranged by the local German authorities, with the services of a German chaplain, a salute fired by a platoon of German soldiers, and a wreath was laid. Sometime later a memorial stone was placed at the site of the crash. 'If you get the chance,' it reads, 'stand quietly by this peaceful stone and, with a little imagination, you too will be able to sense the ripples.'

The attack on Peenemünde caused a delay of two months in research and development. The site was rebuilt, and the Germans fabricated signs of bomb damage by creating dummy craters in the sand and blowing up lightly-damaged buildings. As a result of the attack, an underground V weapon production plant was built in the Harz Mountains. Test launches resumed, and the first V1 fell on England on 13 June 1944, and the first V2 rocket on 8 September.

William Stiles lived in Claverdon and attended King's High in Warwick before arriving at King Edward VI as a day scholar in 1920. A successful sportsman, he was a member of the 1st XV and the 1st XI and was awarded his 2nd XV colours. Eight years later, he joined the offices of a local auctioneer, and by the time that

Stiles, back row, far right.

he joined the Royal Air Force Volunteer Reserve he was a Fellow of the Land Agents Society. He is commemorated in the Memorial Library at King Edward VI School.

The grave of William Stiles in Aabenraa Cemetery.

The Lord bless thee and keep thee
Be gracious unto thee
And give thee peace.
Gravestone of William Stiles, Aabenraa Cemetery, Denmark

Notes
1. RAF Fiskerton was 5 miles east of Lincoln and just north of the village, where the Carpenter's Arms in High Street was a popular haunt of the aircrews.

Chapter 32

KENNETH ALFRED SMITH

Corporal, Royal Air Force Volunteer Reserve
14 September 1943

The pulse of war and passion of wonder,
The heavens that murmur, the sounds that shine,
The stars that sing and the loves that thunder,
The music burning at heart like wine,
An armed archangel whose hands raise up
All senses mixed in the spirit's cup
Till flesh and spirit are molten in sunder –
These things are over, and no more mine.
A.C. Swinburne, *The Triumph of Time*

From its source near the small and picturesque village of Naseby in Northamptonshire, the river Avon winds in a south-westerly direction past the Warwickshire town and villages of Warwick, Barford and Hampton Lucy before reaching Stratford-upon-Avon. For hundreds of years, men have cast their lines. Except in times of flood, the Avon is a slow-moving river, and locals have known the area between Lucy's Mill and Sausage Island as the best places to catch Perch, Tench, Chub and Roach. Kenneth Smith was an excellent angler; it was his particular hobby, and he won many prizes in the local contests. Leaving King Edward VI School in 1930, for which he had been a member of the 1st XV, he contributed regularly to *The Fishing Gazette* and, under the pseudonym 'Ruff and Ready', a regular angling column in the *Stratford-upon-Avon Herald*. Working for his father, a corn and seed dealer in Greenhill Street, Kenneth enjoyed playing cricket for The Early Closers, as well as being part of the thriving table tennis circle in the town. But it was the quietness while fishing by the Avon that he loved most, and this active enthusiasm was simply a natural function of what his family and friends remembered as his moral consciousness.

When war came he joined the Royal Air Force Volunteer Reserve and by 1940 was qualified as an equipment assistant. Posted overseas, he was promoted to corporal and served as an auxiliary driver throughout the North African campaign right through to the victory in Tunisia. On 10 July the British Eighth Army landed at a series of points on the south-eastern coast of Sicily in the Gulf of Noto. A combined operation with the American Seventh Army that lasted six weeks led to the Germans withdrawing the bulk of their forces and supplies across the Straits of Messina to the Italian mainland. Preceded by a massive artillery bombardment of the Italian shore that met little opposition, on 3 September 1943 the Eighth Army crossed the Straits of Messina and established itself in Reggio.

Anticipating trouble in Italy, battle-hardened SS units had been withdrawn from the Eastern Front in July and August, and with troops withdrawn from Sicily, Corsica and Sardinia, the Germans were in control of central Italy when the Italians capitulated and made an armistice with the Allies on 8 September. Ideally suited for defence against an invader planning to move northwards, Italy had *Kenneth Smith.* narrow coast plains on the east and west, cut by many rivers, that flanked the central north-south Apennine Mountains, up almost the whole spine of the country.

Kenneth's death was an unfortunate accident. While supervising the disembarkation of a vehicle from a landing craft on the beach at Reggio, he was operating a braking device on the vehicle when it skidded and threw him against the side of the ship. He died shortly afterwards and was buried in Salerno War Cemetery between Battipaglia and Pontecagnano. In a letter to his parents, Kenneth's commanding officer praised him as a keen and efficient NCO, adding, 'We miss your son, who was such a cheerful and agreeable comrade.' He was twenty-eight.

In Stratford, Kenneth had been associated with the Lodge of the Ancient Order of Druids, and while overseas had held the office of Immediate Post Arch. He is commemorated in the Garden of Remembrance in Old Town, and in the Memorial Library at King Edward VI School.

Here with the stillness of the trees
With the twilight's quietness –
Like stillness to our fears –
A quiet and comfort to our souls.
Richard Spender, *Willow Creek at Sunset*

Notes
1. The Ancient Order of Druids is not a religious organization; rather, its members preserve and practise the main principles attributed to the early Druids, those of justice, benevolence and friendship.
2. The Early Closers was a cricket team whose name came from the time when shops in Stratford closed early on Thursdays.

Chapter 33

WILLIAM ARTHUR LOWTH
Captain, 124 Field Regiment, Royal Artillery
2 November 1943

The shadow of a dove
Falls on the cote, the trees are filled with wings;
F. Scott Fitzgerald, *This Side of Paradise*

In the Congregational Church (now the United Reform Church) in Rother Street there is a lovely and distinctive oak baptismal font that was dedicated by the minister in January 1946. It was presented by Mrs Minerva Lowth in memory of her son, Captain William Lowth, who had died of injuries during the Allied landings in Southern Italy on 2 November 1943. His father John was a solicitor, and his brother Thomas was a captain in the Royal Warwickshire Regiment, who after the war became a solicitor and, for nearly forty years, the Clerk to the Governors of King Edward VI School.

William Lowth.

The brothers had been pupils at the school and had excelled in sports. Both gained colours for the 1st XV, William had been in the 1st XI, whilst Thomas was a rower and succeeded his brother as Captain of Warneford House. Leaving school at Christmas in 1929, William joined Lloyds Bank and played wing-forward for the Long Buckby Rugby Club in Northamptonshire. Moving to the Lloyds branch in Banbury, he became vice-captain of the rugby club there.

At the time of the Munich Crisis in September 1938, as the war clouds gathered William joined the Territorial Army. By the time war was declared a year later, he was a sergeant in the 53 Anti-Tank Corps, which became a section of 124 Field

Regiment, and he went to France in 1939 as part of the British Expeditionary Force. Stationed along the France-Belgium border during the winter and spring, they were driven back by the German advance in May 1940 and evacuated from Dunkirk between 26 May and 4 June. Arriving back in England on 31 May, William, with the regiment, was sent first to Cheshire for reorganization and rest, and then to Blandford Forum in Dorset as part of the anti-invasion plan that covered the coast from Lyme Regis to Christchurch.

With the imminent threat of invasion eased, the regiment was ordered to the Middle East, arriving at Al Qassasin in Egypt on 17 July 1941, and at their final destination in Famagusta, Cyprus, on 5 August.

An expected advance by the Germans into the Caucasus alerted the regiment for a possible move through Palestine to Iraq to join up with the Russians. When the anticipated attack did not come, the regiment spent some time over Christmas in Iraq, until early in the New Year they arrived in Egypt and moved along the coast via Sidi Barrani into Libya.

Like so many of the other Old Boys of the school, as well as the thousands of soldiers, both Allied and Axis, who fought in the Western Desert campaign, it is unlikely that they had ever experienced such a sterile and hostile terrain. Myriad flies plagued them throughout the day and generally clustered so thickly in vehicles that they turned them from brown to black, and the hot wind from the burning deserts of the south spread a blanket of sand over everything, choking the nostrils and mouth, and infiltrating the eyes. Some spoke wistfully of the sunsets, when a coolness came upon the desert and the sky was so beautiful in pastel shades of pink and purple. One piece of desert was like another, a wilderness of repetitions, where great tracts of sterile sand stretched to far horizons.

Throughout the actions in North Africa and the subsequent landing in Sicily and Southern Italy, William participated in the same campaigns as his school friend Kenneth Smith, with the Royal Air Force Volunteer Reserve. He took part in the siege of Tobruk and the Battle of El Alamein, and also when 124 Field Regiment stayed in reserve until the Eighth Army came against the Mareth Line in Tunisia. Then their task was a frontal assault on the line and on into Tripoli.

On 10 July 1943, they landed at Avola, north of Cassibile, in Sicily, and were involved in the Battle of Lentini later that month as both the Italians and Germans retreated to the north of the island. Landing in Southern Italy in September as Staff Captain at Formation Headquarters, he was seriously wounded and died in the 67th Military General Hospital in Naples, overlooking the beautiful bay with the view of the distant Vesuvius, which was to erupt dramatically the following March. William was buried in the Naples War Cemetery, north of the city and on the road to Rome.

William's friends, who regarded him as possessing a rare charm, learned of his death with great sadness, and his old headmaster, the Reverend Cecil Knight, remembered him in the Sunday prayers in the Guild Chapel, as did the Minister of the Congregational Church where for many years William had attended Sunday school. He is commemorated on the Tiddington War Memorial and in the Memorial Library at King Edward VI School.

And down the valley through the crying trees
The body of the darker storm flies
F. Scott Fitzgerald, *This Side of Paradise*

Chapter 34

GEOFFREY FRANCIS CLARK

Flight Sergeant, Pilot, 625 Squadron
24 December 1943

When the siren moan to wake Cologne
They shiver in their shoes;
In the Berlin street they're white as sheets
With a tinge of Prussian blues.
German rhyme

By the beginning of 1943, the tide of the war in Europe was turning against Nazi Germany. Stalingrad had fallen and the Russians had retaken Kursk, Rostov and Kharkov; in North Africa, the Afrika Korps was beginning a series of setbacks; German supply ships were being regularly sunk in the Mediterranean, and Churchill was demanding Germany's unconditional surrender. To a large and carefully selected audience in the Berlin Sportpalast, Propaganda Minister Joseph Goebbels delivered a speech calling for 'Total War'. Although enthusiastically received, the speech was an early admission by the Nazi leadership that Germany faced serious dangers, with its very survival at stake, and exhorted the German people to continue the war even though it would be difficult and long.

Shortly following the Total War speech, Air Marshall Harris told his crews: 'Tonight you go to the Big City, and have an opportunity to light a fire in the belly of the enemy and burn his Black Heart out.' In bombing terms, Berlin was always the big target, the 'Big City', the 'Big B'. For most of the war, it was at the extreme range of Allied aircraft flying from their air bases in East Anglia and the Midlands. At a distance of 600 miles for the night bombers, a return trip under cover of darkness reduced operational possibilities to the winter months between November and March. However, for a number of reasons, Berlin was recognized as one of the most important targets. It was the seat of government, Germany's largest industrial city and the communications hub of the road, rail and canal systems. It was a powerhouse containing dozens of vast armament plants including AEG, Siemens, BMW, Heinkel, Focke-Wulf, Rheinmetall-Borsig and Deutsche Industrie-Werke.

The Battle of Berlin was the longest and most intensive single bombing campaign of the Second World War. Harris had little faith in the complete success of attacks on precise targets, and he made no pretence of simply targeting military installations. The realization of the futility of trying to hit individual buildings at night, through smoke, haze or cloud, was found to be so very inaccurate and was abandoned for a policy of carpet bombing whole areas, although even then the system was prone to failure. However, Harris remained convinced that the bombing of Berlin would end the war: 'It is my belief ... we can push Germany over by bombing this year.' Bombing forced Germany to divide the economy between too many competing claims. In the air over Germany or in the frosts in Russia, German forces lacked the weapons to finish the job.

The experience of the bombing of Berlin was described dramatically by Richard Dimbleby, a BBC correspondent who flew as a civilian observer: 'Over the city there was a complete ring of powerful searchlights, waving and crossing. Also intense flak. When incendiaries were dropped, a dazzling silver pattern spread itself, creating a rectangle of brilliant lights, hundreds, thousands of them, winking and gleaming and lighting the outlines of the city around them. As though this had been a signal, score after score of fire bombs went down and all over the dark face of the city, these great incandescent flowerbeds spread themselves.'

Albert Speer, the German Armaments Minister, recalled: 'The air raids on Berlin were an unforgettable sight, and I had to constantly remind myself of the cruel reality in order not to be completely entranced by the scene: the illumination of the parachute flares, which the Berliners called "Christmas trees", the innumerable probing searchlights, the excitement when a plane was caught and tried to escape the cone of light, the brief flaming torch when it was hit. No doubt about it, this apocalypse provided a magnificent spectacle.'

Following a flight in a Lancaster bomber over Berlin, the American correspondent Edward R. Murrow called it 'a thing of orchestrated hell, a terrible symphony of light and flame'.

Throughout 1943, Lancaster bombers of 625 Squadron flew from RAF Kelstern to Berlin. In the Wolds between Binbrook and Louth, amongst the aircrew who cycled or arranged a car ride over to the The Wheatsheaf in Louth, was Sergeant Geoffrey Clark, the son of a baker on School Hill in Wooten Wawen. A pupil at King Edward VI School between 1931 and 1939, he had been an active participant in the Dramatic Society (appearing in *Vice Versa*), and played occasionally for the 1st XI, being awarded his 2nd XI colours. Becoming a clerk in the Municipal Offices in Birmingham, he travelled each day by train through Henley-in-Arden, Danzey and Earlswood. Joining the Royal Air Force Volunteer Reserve in 1940, he moved to Kelstern, where, from 1941, he was involved in very many raids over German-occupied Europe, 'burning the cities we learned about in school.'

RAF Kelstern Memorial.

On Christmas Eve 1943, the aircrew had received orders for yet another mission against the Big City, and, keyed up like a violin, at the crossroads between life and death, they listened to records played on a wind-up gramophone – *White Christmas*, *I'll be Home for Christmas*, and wistfully sang along to *I'll be seeing you, in all the old familiar places* ... that was so loved by servicemen in the Second World War.

That evening, the four-engine Lancaster Mk III LM421 roared over the fields of flax in Lincolnshire, out over the North Sea and into a gorgeous sunset. Berlin was covered in dense cloud and, wrote Michael Scott, 'the shrieking wind rides high tonight.' The main blows were delivered on the south-eastern districts of Kopenick and Treptow. Of the 364 Lancasters dispatched that night, sixteen failed to return. One was Clark's Lancaster, which was attacked by a German Me 110 Night Fighter piloted by Lieutenant Georg Fenk; it crashed at Mittenwalde in the valley of the river Isar, on the foothills of the Alps. Nine miles from Garmisch-Partenkirchen, from the early seventeenth century it had remained a centre of violin and instrument making.

Four of the crew, including Geoffrey Clark, were buried in Berlin War Cemetery after being exhumed from graves in Mittenwalde. The other three are commemorated on the RAF Memorial at Runnymede.

The decision to go for Berlin over other targets in Germany, such as those that might probably have reduced German fighter strength, was a grave miscalculation. Harris deluded himself in believing that indiscriminate bombing of urban areas provided a war-winning weapon. It did hit Berlin hard, but war production continued until late 1944. The bombing was conducted at a huge cost of life, for by the end of the war, more than 2,500 aircrew had been killed during the attacks on Berlin by Bomber Command. They were brave, intelligent and technically skilled young men who could have contributed so much to the recovery of Britain after the war. Instead, the majority lie in the military cemetery established by the British occupation authorities and the Commonwealth War Graves Commission on the south side of Heerstrasse in Charlottenburg.

Geoffrey Clark is commemorated on the Wooten Wawen War Memorial, which stands by the A34 road to Stratford-upon-Avon, in the Roll of Honour in St Peter's Church in Wooten Wawen, and in the Memorial Library at King Edward VI School.

> *Lie in the dark and listen*
> *Hundreds of them, thousands perhaps,*
> *It's clear tonight so they're flying high,*
> *Riding the icy, moonlit sky.*
>
> *Lie in the dark and let them go,*
> *Lie in the dark and listen...*
> Terence Rattigan, *Flare Path*

Commonwealth War Graves, Berlin.

Chapter 35

ROWLAND HENRY MEGAINEY
Pilot Officer, 433 Squadron
22 January 1944

Listen, listen can you hear
That whispered sound so very slight
And feel again a long shed fear
Rex Polendine, *Place of Ghosts*

The development of technological innovation in the campaigns of both Bomber Command and the Luftwaffe is a story of imagination and initiative. By the early months of 1941, the Germans had established an integrated defensive system that comprised searchlights, flak and night fighters. To counter this, some of the British bombers carried a device that enabled them to jam the German radar. Also, a microphone was fitted into the engine bay of a bomber that recorded the loud engine roar, which the wireless operator transmitted on the German ground-to-air frequencies. This made it impossible for night fighters to speak to their controllers. In addition, German-speaking RAF pilots tuned into the radio frequency of the Luftwaffe night fighters and gave misleading instructions.

The battle of wits continued as the losses of Bomber Command climbed to alarming and very critical levels. Then, in 1943, a brilliant scientific device was introduced that would confuse the German radar operators and 'fog' all their screens. Codenamed 'Window', it consisted of bundles of thin metallized foil strips that were dropped at intervals during a bomber's run, creating confusing signals on German radar screens and concealing the actual position of the bombers. The Germans had thought of a similar device but never used it.

The new device was used first on the raid on Hamburg on 24 July 1943 with dramatic effect. Searchlights wandered across the sky and the city's fifty-six heavy and thirty-six light flak batteries were firing desperate barrages, helpless in their inability to take radar predictions on the aircraft above. The night fighters failed to locate the bomber traffic, showing that the German ground controllers were utterly confused as their radar service suggested an attack by 11,000 bombers. The raid was an overwhelming success and the hedges, houses and farmland of North Germany were littered with foil strips like errant Christmas decorations, being chewed by cows and draped over telegraph wires.

The German scientists understood the significance of Windows and for a time had no answer. But not for long. Early in 1943, the Luftwaffe had created the Wild Boar squadrons. These were single-engined fighters that were vectored into the bomber streams over the target by a radio running commentary from information obtained by observer posts all over Germany. Now 'Tame Boar' was developed, in which twin-engined night fighters were directed onto individual bombers by the controllers as soon as the approximate course of the bomber force was

Rowland Megainey.

known. In the final stages of interception, the air turbulence created by hundreds of bombers warned the fighters. On a clear night they could search visually and in moonless conditions they relied on radar. By early 1944, the German A1 radar had become impervious to Windows. At the same time, a lighter coloured night fighter broke up its shape in moonlight and became very effective.

The British bomber had always had a blind spot, and it had not taken the Luftwaffe long to find it, although it was not until late 1943 that the solution was found, when an ingenious fitter at a Luftwaffe airfield devised the prototype of the deadly 'Schrage Musik' (Jazz Music). A pair of fixed upward-firing 20mm cannon were mounted behind the fighter's cockpit. The pilot flew unseen beneath the bomber and fired a short burst into the inner wing structure, which destroyed the main spa and ripped the wing from the bomber, sending it out of control. These changes in tactics came in time to help the Germans to counter the main night offensive of Bomber Command. German crews were ordered to pursue the bombers to the absolute limit of their endurance, and once they had made contact to only break off when their fuel was almost gone.

Receiving the latest position, height, course and strength of a bomber stream, the night fighters were assigned as close to the stream as possible, and as many as fifty fighters circled in the darkness waiting to select a target and pounce. These were the tactics employed by the Luftwaffe as 433 Squadron was formed as a heavy bomber unit of 6 (Royal Canadian Air Force) Group at Skipton-on-Swale in the Vale of York, on 25 September 1943. Adopted by the Porcupine District of Northern Ontario, the squadron operated with the Halifax B111, and its first mission was laying mines in the area of the Frisian Islands (a series of islands that stretched from the north-west of The Netherlands, through Germany to the west of Denmark), and bombing Berlin on 18 January 1944.

Rowland Megainey, the son of farmers Frank and Daisy Megainey who lived on the Shipston Road, left King Edward VI School in July 1940 to join his father as a farmer, where he remained until 1943, when he enlisted in the Royal Air Force Volunteer Reserve. After attending the Officer Training Unit in Stratford-upon-Avon, he crewed up and was ordered to RAF Skipton-on-Swale towards the end of the year.

On the night of 20 January, the seven-man crew of Halifax Mk III HX289 took off for a raid on Berlin. The approach route took a wide swing to the north, but the diversion did not deceive the Germans, and the controllers on the ground managed to feed the night fighters into the bomber stream. The area over Berlin was completely cloud-covered, preventing any photographic reconnaissance, and what bombing there was fell on eastern parts of the city. In retaliation Hitler ordered raids the following night against London and Southern England.

Megainey and the crew flew again on 21 January, taking off at 8.00 pm for the first major raid on Magdeburg. The German controller once again followed the progress of the 648 bomber stream across the North Sea, and many night fighters

RAF Runnymeade Memorial.

– showing the success of the Tame Boar tactics – were in the stream before it crossed the German coast. The fighters scored steadily before the bombers turned for home.

The last message from HX289 was received when 50 miles over the North Sea, reporting that its starboard outer engine was gone. All members of the crew were lost, and they are commemorated on the RAF Memorial at Runneymede. It was a bad night for Bomber Command, losing fifty-seven aircraft.

Rowland Megainey is commemorated in the Garden of Remembrance in Old Town, and also in the Memorial Library at King Edward VI School.

> *Surely I am not alone*
> *To sense and feel the pulsing air*
> *And now a rising higher tone*
> *And look I see them over there*
> Rex Polendine, *Place of Ghosts*

Notes
1. Sir Arthur Harris had originally presented the idea of the bombing campaign by declaring that while it would cost 500 bombers, 'it will cost Hitler the war.' The reality was that the great night battles between 18 November 1943 and 31 March 1944 resulted in the loss of 1,047 aircraft.

Chapter 36

FREDERICK JOHN BAILEY

Warrant Officer, Pilot, 73 Squadron
20 February 1944

Sleep is the innocent, harmless joy of men
Who, troubled and weighed down by many cares
No other comfort know
Geoffrey Bond, *The Death of Each Day's Life*

A new class of reserve was created in August 1936, when the Royal Air Force Volunteer Reserve was established in a series of 'Town Centres', where ground instruction was given, and 'Aerodrome Centres' near the towns, where flying was taught by civilian schools. To fulfil the need for 500 pilots a year, there was a Pilot Section, plus sections for training mechanics. Twenty-two Aerodrome Centres were set up, which included thirteen civilian schools already training RAF pilots. This gave young men between eighteen and twenty-five the chance to learn to fly in their spare time. Receiving £25 a year, they attended a fifteen-day flying course at one of the training centres. It was very popular, and there was great enthusiasm, so that by the time war was declared in September 1939, there were 2,500 RAFVR pilots in training.

Frederick Bailey in the 1st XV.

The son of a farmer on Atherstone Hill near Preston-on-Stour, Frederick Bailey had attended the little village school before joining King Edward VI School between 1934 and 1938, where his friends included David Overbury and Philip Lomas. Joining the RAFVR in 1940, Frederick trained as a pilot, reached the rank of warrant officer, and was posted to 73 Squadron, which from October 1943 was operating the Spitfire Mk V in Italy and the Balkans and based at Foggia Main, just north of Bari. A city of some 250,000 people, Bari had an attractive section of houses from the Middle Ages that clustered around a promontory that jutted into the Adriatic Sea.

Little thought had been given to the possibility of a German air raid on Bari. Allied leaders believed the Luftwaffe in Italy to be so weak and stretched so thin that it was incapable of mounting a major effort. But the Germans needed to stop the northward advance of the Allied armies, and as the port of Bari appeared critical to their supply line, the Germans hoped that by bombing and destroying the port they would stall the Allied advance.

Not everyone in Bari was sure that the Luftwaffe was a spent force, and they expressed serious reservations that preparation for a possible attack were so inadequate. On the afternoon of 2 December 1943, a Messerschmitt Me 210 reconnaissance plane flew over the port. Cruising at 23,000 feet in a clear, blue sky, it was very visible, but the anti-aircraft crews took little notice.

At dusk that evening, the docks were brilliantly lit as cranes stood out in sharp relief as they unloaded cargo from American, British, Polish, Norwegian and Dutch ships. In addition to the usual war material, they carried aviation fuel for bombers and other much needed supplies to support Allied forces engaged in the battle for Rome. That evening, about 200 officers, fifty-two civilian technicians and several hundred enlisted men from the airfields at Foggia were in Bari.

At 7.25 pm, three German aircraft circled the harbour, soon followed by 100 Junkers Ju 88s. Most of the planes came from Italian airfields, for the Germans wanted to use a few aircraft flying from Yugoslavia in the hope that the Allies would believe that the entire mission had originated from there, and therefore misdirect any retaliatory strikes. The Ju 88s were ordered to fly east to the Adriatic, then swing south-west. Surprise was total. The air defences were caught out completely as the Ju 88s dropped their bombs. In moments, the harbour was blazing with burning ships.

A bulk petrol pipeline on a quay was severed, the gushing fuel ignited and a sheet of burning fuel spread over much of the harbour and engulfed those ships not yet damaged. Ships were in various stages of burning or sinking, and then the flames reached holds full of munitions and exploded. The surface of the water was covered by a viscous scum of oil and fuel, blinding and choking those unlucky to be in the water.

One of the destroyed ships had been carrying a secret cargo of 2,000 First World War mustard gas bombs that had been sent to Europe to retaliate if Germany had resorted to chemical warfare. The destruction of the vessel caused liquid sulphur mustard from the bombs to spill into waters already contaminated by oil from the other ships. So the malevolent cargo was turned against the Allies themselves.

In 1943 there was a real possibility that the Germans may use poison gas. Germany was on the defensive on all fronts, and the Allies were now in Europe and slowly advancing up the Italian peninsula. Although not a great advocate of chemical warfare, Hitler was nevertheless ruthless and could be persuaded that using poison gas could redress the balance of the war in his favour.

The bombing of Bari.

Very fortunately, there were a number of Allied military hospitals with support systems in Bari, and casualties from the raid began to pour in. Swamped with wounded of all types and still not realizing that they were dealing with poison gas, the hospital staff allowed the victims to remain in their oil and gas-soaked clothes. As the victims began to die, the doctors began to suspect that some kind of chemical agent was involved. By the end of the year, eighty-three of the 628 hospitalized victims had died.

At first, the Allied High Command concealed the disaster in case the Germans believed that the Allies were preparing to use chemical weapons and provoke them to use them. Officially, sixty-nine deaths were attributed in whole or part to the mustard gas, although more than 1,000 Allied servicemen and more than 1,000 Italian civilians were caught up in the maelstrom of the acrid fumes. Frederick Bailey was in Bari that night, and on 20 February 1944 he died in the 98th General Hospital.

The offensive launched in January 1944 was part of the overall push that included the Anglo-American landings at Anzio. Elements crossed the Rapido River and established a bridgehead, but were forced to withdraw due to the lack of supplies. The official explanation was bad weather, but the closing of Bari because of the attack the previous December was very probably the major reason.

Frederick Bailey was buried in the Bari War Cemetery near Carbonara, and is commemorated in the Garden of Remembrance in Stratford-upon-Avon and in the Memorial Library at King Edward VI School.

You are beneath
You are in air
You are in earth
You are beside me
You are within
Italian prayer

Notes

1. Secrecy shrouded the affair at Bari. The cargo of mustard gas bombs was not only controversial but also embarrassing. On the orders of Allied leaders, records were destroyed and the whole affair remained a secret. American records were declassified in 1959, but the episode remained obscure until 1967. It was not until 1986 that the British Government admitted to the event. The secrecy may have caused additional deaths because if the presence of mustard gas had been known, more victims, especially civilians, may have sought proper treatment.

Chapter 37

ARTHUR JAMES COGBILL

Flying Officer, 1658 Heavy Conversion Unit
22 March 1944

In the shadow of thy wings ...
Will I rejoice.
Gravestone in All Saint's Churchyard, Honington

Following the road to London out of Stratford-upon-Avon taken 400 years ago by another Old Boy of King Edward VI School, the traveller passes through the villages of Alderminster and Newbold-on-Stour, until just beyond Tredington there is a lane on the left that winds over a five-arched seventeenth-century bridge to the gated village of Honington. It is one of the most beautiful villages in the Cotswolds, with a particular charm and gentility, where apple trees flourish in gardens and the surrounding fields. Immediately south-east of the Caroline Honington Hall is the Church of All Saints, where tall yew and grey poplar trees embrace the entrance to the churchyard. Within a few steps and on the left side there is the grave of Arthur Cogbill, with its Commonwealth War Graves Commission headstone. It is a solitary and secluded spot. The graves of his father, a farm labourer on the Honington Estate, and his mother lie further up on the right.

Whilst generations of his family had attended the small village school before working in the fields, Arthur was the first member to go to a grammar school when he was given a free place at King Edward VI School between 1919 and 1926. *The Stratfordian* records his participation as 'a speedy wing' with the 1st XV – he was awarded 2nd XV colours, success in the 1st IX, becoming a prefect, and the contribution of a number of articles and stories to the school magazine that were both erudite and beguiling. Language was certainly his strength, so when he left school to study at the University of Birmingham, it was in English that he was awarded first his BA and then an MA.

In the years that followed, when he was in the Stratford area, he played regularly for the Old Edwardians XV, a group of younger players that split from the more robust Town XV. He also enjoyed cricket and golf, and in the season of

Arthur Cogbill, seated cross-legged, 2nd from right, in the Old Edwardians XV, 1938.

1938 he won the Avon Tennis Club Cup. In 1935 he had moved to Morpeth in Northumberland to teach at the Girls' High School, and in 1938 to Bedlington Grammar School, 10 miles from Newcastle. Arthur was popular at Bedlington, becoming producer of the school dramatic society, and he brought several groups of Berwick and Bedlington schoolboys to Honington to help with the harvest and fruit picking. In his memory several years following his death, the school introduced the Arthur J. Cogbill Memorial Prize for the best spoken English. It was awarded annually until the Grammar School was closed in the 1970s.

Memorial prize certificate.

Arthur became captain of the local Home Guard when it was established in Bedlington in early 1940. At school he had been a member of the Cadet Corps and at university a platoon sergeant in the Officer Training Corps (OTC), and with effect from 28 February 1941, he was granted a commission 'for the duration of the hostilities' with the Air Training Corps (ATC) Training Branch of the RAFVR. Joining the RAF in February 1943, he relinquished his commission, becoming a pilot officer. He was posted to Edinburgh, then RAF Montrose, before arriving at RAF Ricall, 9 miles south of York, in late 1943. Here a Halifax Conversion Unit had been created by the merging of a number of conversion units to form C Flight 1658, with a full strength of thirty-two Halifax Mk IIs. The introduction of the large heavy bomber had created many problems, as it required more men to operate it, and two additional members – a mid-upper gunner and a flight engineer – were added to each aircrew. This meant that a further stage of training had to be introduced and the newly formed aircrews had, on leaving the OTUs, to be 'converted' to a larger and more complicated aircraft.

Airfields had to be enlarged and extended, as too were the workshops and power plants that were redesigned to service larger bombers. Initially there was a shortage of trained radar mechanics and bomb handlers, and these had to be trained in order to deal with the new bombers.

Arthur became a flying officer with the responsibility of training crews, many of whom were members of the Royal Canadian Air Force, and four of them were among the crew of eight that took off from Ricall for a training flight in Halifax Mk II W7865 on 22 March 1944.

Arthur Cogbill's grave in Honington.

What precisely happened is unclear, but as the dependability of the Halifax had always been highly suspect and the fact that seventy-two of them were lost during the time that the unit was at Ricall, a major malfunction is likely. At 9.47 pm, W7865 crashed near Cattal Station just beyond the lovely village of Kirk Hammerton on the York to Knaresborough railway line. The Canadian pilot, Peter Banks, was killed, and the rest of the crew injured. Taken to Naburn Military Hospital, near York, Arthur Cogbill died later that evening. His funeral at All Saints Church was attended by many friends, including the headmaster of Bedlington School and officers from RAF Ricall. There are squadron and unit memorials at all the RAF stations where he served, and he is commemorated in All Saint's Church in Honington and in the Memorial Library at King Edward VI School.

> *Speak the speech, I pray you, as I pronounc'd it to you,*
> *trippingly on the tongue, but if you mouth it, as many*
> *of our players do, I had as life the town-crier spoke my lines.*
> William Shakespeare, *Hamlet*, Act III Scene II

Chapter 38

GORDON ROBERT COLLINS
Sergeant, 622 Squadron
31 March 1944

They beg, order, are not heard; and hear the darker
Voice rising: Can't you hear me? Over. Over –
All the air quivers, and the east sky glows.
Randall Jarrell, *The Front*

By the spring of 1944, the campaign of bombing Germany had grown in intensity, in ferocity and in the enormous human cost to Bomber Command. Crews flew regularly, over long distances, usually at night, and too often with insufficient rest between missions. They became 'a family in arms', a mutually dependent team, and each man contributed to the survival of the others, and to the success of an operation. Although the pilot, navigator and the bomb-aimer were considered the 'brains' of the crew, and the wireless operator, the flight engineer and the two gunners were the 'tradesmen', they considered themselves all equal and there was a genuine comradeship. They all lived under great stress and after so many missions they

Gordon Collins.

became somewhat fatalistic, but were sustained to a large extent by the strength of the crew. Superstitions were strong. Some prayed, some had talismans, and some followed rituals before flying.

After all the checks were complete, the green light was received for take-off, and the bomber climbed to the designated rendezvous point. In darkness, with many other aircraft at the same altitude and in the bomber stream, the aircraft flew with no navigation light. The only way they knew whether there were other aircraft around was by flying through another bomber's slipstream. The possibility of collision was a constant fear. Aircraft were scheduled to arrive over the target in waves two minutes apart and at various heights. But bombers were often late in arriving or were not at their allotted height, whether because of mechanical or navigational problems. Now dozens of probing searchlights found them, and there was the continuous barrage of anti-aircraft shells in an area that was thick with heavy bombers. Often at about the same height there would be a flash of light that then slowly faded. The pilots were unable to manoeuvre the controls of the tumbling aircraft. Another collision, another fourteen airmen gone.

In 1941, Gordon Collins joined the Fleet Air Arm of the Royal Navy, which had been formed in April 1924, and when war was declared in 1939 it consisted of twenty squadrons with a total of 232 aircraft. His time there was short and by the end of the year he had transferred to the Royal Air Force Volunteer Reserve and been posted as an air gunner to 622 Squadron at RAF Mildenhall. Many of the young airmen in the RAFVR had been sportsmen at school, educated above the average, spoke confidently and had a great interest in flying.

At King Edward VI School, Gordon had been a member of a 1st XV that contained Rogers Miller, Richard Spender and James Overbury, and had joined the local Air Training Corps before securing a position in the Treasury in Great George Street in Whitehall. At Mildenhall, having crewed up, he took part in many

Gordon seated, far right.

148

training flights, and later a number of combat missions over Occupied Europe through 1943 that preceded his involvement in the infamous Nuremberg Raid on Friday, 31 March 1944. Sir Arthur Harris decided that here was a large, virtually intact, industrial target in just the right place.

Nuremberg had great political significance. Architecturally it was important because it contained many beautiful churches and medieval buildings, including the studio of Albrecht Dürer, and it was rich in imperial history. Hitler had declared that Nuremberg was the most German of German cities. Every September between 1933 and 1938, the Nazis had held their week-long gatherings and party rallies in the vast stadiums south-east of the city centre. For Harris, it was 'the large target'.

Once the decision had been made, a great deal depended on the weather. The bombers were to take off late in the evening, so that their arrival over Nuremberg while the moon was up would be kept to a minimum. Part of the plan was also to avoid the defences in the Ruhr and to take a wide sweep over Northern Germany before turning south, and so conceal from the Germans the identity of the target.

During that Thursday, the crews had been waiting for the telephone to alert them to an operation, and from the moment they knew the target there was a peculiar atmosphere of suspense, because it was to be a moonlit night with no cloud cover. They also knew that it was a grim target and that many of them would not come back. At 10.30 pm, Lancaster ND767 roared down the runway at Mildenhall. Piloted by Flying Officer Picken, the seven-man crew was experienced but nervous. As they crossed the Belgian coast and reached the designated point for turning, the bombers began to lose their compact formation as the winds changed their alignment. They also became aware of the presence of German night fighters in strength, with two hours' fuel in their tanks, and in the clearest weather conditions under a brilliant half-moon. Due to some unusual and unfortunate quirk in the weather, vapour and condensation trails started to appear behind each bomber.

Bomber crews had always been told to find and bomb their targets and then do their utmost to get their precious bombers home. On this night the winds took most of the bombers away from their main target, adding confusion for the navigators. In consequence, damage to Nuremberg was limited, and as the bombers turned away for the return journey, the fighters continued in pursuit. Having dropped their bombs, the bombers were more manoeuvrable but still very vulnerable. Caught by anti-aircraft fire and the fighters, many bombers exploded and the flames lit up other bombers in silhouette.

Forty miles off track and in the middle of a leg almost 300 miles in length, the pilot of a Halifax from 247 Squadron, advised by his navigator that he was off-course, made a slight course alteration. Too late, he saw Lancaster ND767 immediately above him. Yelling, 'What the hell?' there was a terrific crash as the two aircraft collided. The Lancaster went into a nosedive and plunged into the ground near Rachecourt in Luxembourg. The rear gunner of the Halifax managed to escape by parachute and was the only man in either crew to survive. Gordon and the rest of the Lancaster crew were buried in Hotton War Cemetery in Luxembourg.

'Failure cries out for explanation but success, like charity, covers a multitude of error,' wrote Erwin Rommel. The Nuremberg Raid was a tragic failure, and the cost to the crews was high. Of the 795 aircraft that took off on 30 March, sixty-four Lancasters and thirteen Halifaxes were lost. For some months, Gordon and his crew were listed as 'missing from air operations', but on 15 December, the *Stratford-upon-Avon Herald* announced that he was 'presumed killed'. He is commemorated in the Garden of Remembrance in Old Town and in the Memorial Library at King Edward VI School.

High in the sunlit silence hovering there,
I've chased the shouting wind along,
And flung my eager craft through footless halls of air.
John Gillespie Magee, *High Flight*

Chapter 39

FREDERICK CHARLES PINFOLD
Sergeant, Air Gunner, 158 Squadron
13 April 1944

until the break of day
And the shadows flee away.
Gravestone in St Helen Churchyard, Clifford Chambers

Patrick Bishop wrote in *Bomber Boys* that there was no system that could take the danger out of learning how to operate a bomber. Bomber crews had an intimate relationship with death, which shadowed them from the first months of training. Night flying particularly was a vital skill, but presented any number of hazards in training. Non-combat crashes accounted for 15 per cent of fatalities, and the very pointlessness of these losses made them stick in the mind. Crashes affected morale, because lives had been lost for nothing, and too often in clapped-out and underserviced aircraft. By the end of the war, 8,090 Bomber Command personnel had been killed in training accidents, and there was great anger because of the suspicion that many of these deaths had been avoidable. It was also during the winter of 1943 that morale amongst aircrews slipped dangerously, and the leadership of Bomber Command failed to see the signs. The line between surviving or not was becoming very thin.

Frederick Pinfold was the son of a postman in Clifford Chambers, and after attending the local village school moved to King Edward VI, where his friends included Geoffrey Cross, Rogers Miller and James Overbury. When he left school he worked at the Shakespeare Memorial Theatre (now the Royal Shakespeare Theatre) in the seasons directed by Iden Payne, with casts that regularly included Donald Wolfit, Alec Clunes and John Laurie, and notable productions including *King Lear*, *Coriolanus* and *Hamlet*. Remaining there until 1940, he enlisted in the Royal Air Force Volunteer Reserve, trained as an air gunner and flew on a number of missions over Germany and Occupied Europe. Targets included Duisburg, Hanover and Peenemünde. In 1943 he joined No. 4 Group 158 Squadron and was ordered to the 1663 Heavy Conversion Unit at RAF Rufforth, 4 miles west of York. It was quite close to where Arthur Cogbill had been stationed and the Tankard Inn in Rufforth was popular with aircrew. A sub-station

Healaugh, Swaledale.

of RAF Marston Moor, the unit would convert crews coming from Operational Training Units whose previous experience had only been on twin-engined aircraft, to fly the large four-engined Halifax bomber. Yorkshire was home to about forty airfields during the Second World War and a good number of them were in the Vale of York. At the edge of the Hambleton Hills the Vale spread towards the Yorkshire Dales, and aircrews checked their bearings by the White Horse carved in the chalk.

More than 18,000 airmen died flying from Yorkshire airfields and a significant number of some of these were lost on training flights, either because of aircraft malfunction or weather conditions. Eighteen Halifaxes were lost on operations from RAF Rufforth, and one of these was Halifax Mk V EB204.

Taking off for another night exercise, it crashed within a minute amongst trees in the small village of Healaugh, south-west of the airfield in Swaledale. In the wreckage of the smashed Halifax five of the crew were killed, including Frederick Pinfold. He was twenty-three and was brought home to be buried in St Helen's Churchyard, not far from the village school in Clifford Chambers, and is commemorated on the village war memorial and in the Memorial Library at King Edward VI School.

we remember your faces eternally young.
John Kent, *Yes, We Remember*

Notes
1. RAF Rufforth is now the site of the York Gliding Club, and the old control tower still stands.

Frederick's grave in Clifford Chambers.

War memorial at Clifford Chambers.

Chapter 40

PHILIP EDWIN LOMAS

Sergeant, Navigator, Royal Air Force Volunteer Reserve
21 April 1944

When the lights go on again all over the world
And the boys are home again all over the world.
Eddie Seiler, Sol Marcus and Bennie Benjeman, *When the Lights Go On Again*

Popular music is tied with nostalgia and collective memory. During the Second World War there was a unique connection between music and upon its acute relationship to warfare, for servicemen stationed overseas, and for mothers, wives and girlfriends waiting at home. There was a strong sentimentality, but also the music was able to cheer and entertain. Whether in mess halls, factories, at home by the fire, or where servicemen were able to find often fleeting relaxation, popular music reflected the feelings of hope, despair, absence and loss. Gramophone records and eventually the BBC made the music available, and on pianos in dozens of bars and public houses close to airfields, young men beat out Glenn Miller's version of *In the Mood* or wistfully played *Always in my Heart* or *If I had My Way*. Seventy years later, the music continues to give perspective to those crucial years.

Terence Joy had enjoyed playing his guitar at home in Shipston-on-Stour and later in an RAF dance band. His great friend at King Edward VI School was Philip Lomas, a warm hearted boy from Tredington, and they joined the school in the same September, in 1931, as Rogers Miller, Geoffrey Cross, James Overbury, Frederick Pinfold and Robert Holder. Leaving in 1939, Philip joined the Shipston Rural District Council (close to the boundaries of Gloucestershire and Oxfordshire in the northern part of the Cotswolds) as a Rating and Valuation Officer. When the Home Guard – initially called the Local Defence Volunteers – was established in May 1940, Philip joined the local unit in Shipston. To begin with, only one man in six had a rifle, and they trained in the evenings on unarmed combat and simple sabotage. Later that summer Philip volunteered for the Royal Air Force, and as part of the British Commonwealth Training Plan he was sent to Canada, where he qualified as a navigator at the Port Arthur Air Navigation School, at the township of Ashfield-Colbourne-Wawanosh in Huron County, in Ontario. President Roosevelt referred to Canada as 'the aerodrome of democracy'. It was a wonderful place to train, with such wide open spaces so suitable for flying and navigation training. Returning to England he participated in missions over Occupied Europe, and in late 1943 as a member of a tour-expired aircrew he was sent to 30 Operational Training Unit at RAF Seighford, 4 miles north-west of Stafford. Many evenings they would relax in The Hollybush in Stafford.

Piloted by Flying Officer Ernest Barrett, Wellington Mk III BK347 took off from RAF Hixon, 7 miles from Stafford, at 10.40 am for a routine cross-country navigational exercise. With dense cloud throughout the flight, Philip found it difficult to establish the correct position of the Wellington and to maintain their course. The pilot and crew decided to descend below the cloud base in an attempt to establish their position. Unknown to them they were flying 150 miles off course and over the high ground of the North Yorkshire Moors. At 4.15 pm, as descending through the cloud, the aircraft ploughed into the eastern face of Whernside (one of the three Yorkshire peaks). All the crew except the tail gunner, the 'Tail-End Charlie', were killed.

Philip was buried in the same grave as his father, who had died in 1939, and lies in a quiet corner of the cemetery in Shipston. The funeral was attended by friends from his squadron, members of the Home Guard, the District Council and

Whernside.

The grave of Philip Lomas in Shipston-on-Stour.

more than fifty wreaths covered his grave. The *Evesham Journal* reported the death of 'a fine type of young Englishman, quiet and retiring'. Philip is commemorated on the Shipston-on-Stour War Memorial, the Tredington War Memorial, and in the Memorial Library at King Edward VI School.

> *now, behind the stars, beyond all sweetness,*
> *Hid in the heart of music, voiced in song,*
> *They are ours*
> A.J.P. Herbert

Notes

1. The site of the crash is frequently visited, and the scar of the impact is still visible. Over the years much of the wreckage has been removed but a few scraps of metal remain. The three Yorkshire peaks are Whernside, Ingleborough and Pen-y-ghent.

2. The tail gunner, Sergeant Joseph Marks, who survived the crash on Whernside, was killed in October 1944 when the aircraft in which he was a tail gunner crashed on the Dutch-German border.

3. Several of the wartime buildings at RAF Seighford, including the Control Tower and the Operations and Crew Briefing remain.

Chapter 41

CHARLES HARRY ODELL

Sapper, 59 Field Company, Royal Engineers
11 May 1944

The air around Cassino was described by the poet
H. Brennan as 'a moth-dusted mist'

In the spring of 1944, Charles Odell of the Royal Engineers took the old Route 6 north of Naples through the Liri Valley to the little town of Cassino, with the rivers Gari and Rapido. Much of the mountainside was thickly wooded with olive, wild oak, fir and acacia. Elsewhere it was terraced with small patches of corn and vine. At that time the whole mountain was covered with ginestra, the beautiful and vicious yellow-flowering bloom. 'On the summit,' wrote Fred Majdalany in his book *The Battle of Cassino*, 'the tranquillity was tangible, the silence almost audible.' The Abbey of Monte Cassino was founded by St Benedict in AD 529, and it was there that during the last eighteen years of his life, his ideas reached fulfilment, he wrote his guide to organization and government that became the blueprint for Western monasticism, and the first community of the Benedictine Order came into being. Forty years after Benedict's death, the monastery suffered the first of its four destructions when the Lombards sacked it. Rebuilt in AD 717, it was the Saracens that destroyed it in AD 883, and in AD 953 it was again rebuilt and entered a golden period of influence when the monks began to transcribe the glorious works of ancient literature. To the monks, history owes Varro's *De Lingua Latina* and the works of Horace, Cicero, Virgil and Ovid. An earthquake wrecked the monastery in 1349, but it was rebuilt once more. It later enjoyed a further flowering during the Renaissance as a centre for artists. In 1944, the monastery lay again in the path of war, and this time it was to suffer its greatest destruction. 'Benedict's monastery,' wrote Fred Majdalany, 'had to die in order that his ideals might have another chance to survive in a world that had largely abandoned them.'

Charles Odell and Patrick Overton were childhood friends who joined King Edward VI School in September 1929, but by midsummer 1942, as a trainee pilot in the United States, Patrick had been killed in an accident. The war had exerted a heavy price on friendships, and each loss had been mourned by the headmaster in the Sunday service in the Guild Chapel, where the boys had attended each school morning.

Charles was an enthusiastic member of the 1st XV and was awarded 2nd XV Colours, before leaving school in July 1933 to join the engineering company F. Ballance. He enlisted in the Army when war was declared in September 1939. By early 1940, he was in the Royal Engineers, and with 59 Company became part of the Middle East Command forces when in September the Italians in Cyrenaica crossed the Egyptian border. Advancing to Sidi Barrani, they halted to await reinforcements before resuming their planned advance on Cairo. This action was the beginning of a succession of advances and retreats that marked the war in the Western Desert. Early campaigns led to British victory and Italian defeat, before there was a reversal of fortune with the arrival of the German Afrika Korps in March 1941.

All during the campaign in the Western Desert, although the Royal Engineers fulfilled its role of constructing defences, building bridges and removing obstacles, they used a great deal of their resources and energies supplying water, camouflage, mine defences and clearance, and built airfields.

Water was vital because of the arid conditions in the desert, and so 59 Field Company when advancing, as with so many other engineers, located and dug wells, cleaned the water, installed pumps, established storage facilities and lay water pipes. All this was dismantled and wells destroyed when the Army had to retreat. Because concealing forces in the wide open spaces of the desert was extremely difficult, the engineers created imaginative deceptions that successfully convinced German intelligence: dummy tanks, lorries and pipelines. Advanced landing grounds were provided because of the growing significance of the RAF during the campaign, and during the siege of Tobruk the engineers constructed an underground hangar.

Because of the featurelessness of the Western Desert, it was ideal for the use of mines, thousands of them, in a defensive role. Experience gained from both the laying and clearing of mines saw the creation of a Royal Engineers School of Mines, where Sappers learned the skill of detecting and clearing. With this experience they successfully cleared routes through German minefields in preparation for the battle of El Alamein. This thorough preparation, which also included water facilities, enabled the British Eighth Army to break through the German defences, and the Sappers to destroy enemy tanks and guns and to render them useless for any future use. Following this victory, 59 Field Company accompanied other companies of the Royal Engineers as the Allied army swept through to Tunisia and victory in the desert by May 1943.

On 10 July, 59 Field Company landed with the combined Anglo-American invasion of Sicily, providing all the necessary facilities including bridges, road repairs and airfields for the advancing troops until the island was secured later in August.

The Germans did not seriously oppose the landings at Reggio in Southern Italy, deciding instead to establish a series of strong lines of defence at strategic areas across the country, including the Gustav Line and the Gothic Line. Because of the nature of the countryside the Sappers had many obstacles to clear, bridges and airfields to construct, mines to clear, and water and electricity supplies to establish. The pace of the Allied advance was causing heavy congestion on all the supply routes, and heavy bridging equipment – so very necessary in an area with so many canals – was difficult to bring forward on the dust-laden roads. Italy was a country ideally suited for defence. No sooner had one river or mountain barrier been crossed than another barred the way.

In many respects the dust was worse than the sand they had endured in North Africa. Nothing was safe against it; the troops ate dust-covered food and drank water that was heavily laced with the stuff.

Then they arrived at the entrance to the Liri Valley, north of Naples, which was dominated by Monte Cassino, and behind it rose, in the words of historian John Ellis, 'a vile tactical puzzle'. So very sudden and theatrical, its appearance had the impression that it reached out for the sole purpose of menace. It was one of the strongest natural defensive positions in military history, and the Germans were in

Amazon bridge.

Monte Cassino in ruins, 1944.

place and waiting. The area suited delaying tactics, and a number of ferocious attacks and counter-attacks in January and February 1944 cost huge losses on both sides, and on 15 February, the monastery was systematically turned to piles of rubble by heavy bombers. Two days later, German paratroopers occupied ruins that had been turned into more protective defensive positions and a major German observation point. Further Allied attacks were both unsuccessful and with very great losses. The Germans too paid a heavy price, but their Gustav Line still held.

Such attrition was the quintessential ordeal of infantry fighting, and it was unavoidable when a well positioned and determined enemy was prepared to defend to the death the ground he holds.

A major obstacle to the Allied advance was the Rapido River, and the construction of a bridge by 59 Field Company would allow for a breakthrough, although the area was in direct view of the Germans, and the company suffered many losses. The morning of 11 May was unusually cloudy and a little rain fell; even the desolation of war did not prevent the countryside from looking beautiful, and the whole valley was soft and green with poppies growing.

An evening construction and crossing was planned, and just before the moon rose there was total darkness for the completion of the bridge that was planned to be completed by 2.00 am, allowing for the first assault. The Germans, however, could see what was happening, and blanketed the river with heavy smoke, which caused confusion as the Sappers' visibility was less than 2 feet. In the midst of this blinding smoke there was constant German machine-gun and mortar fire. The cost for 59 Field Company was high, and amongst the Sappers killed during the night was Charles Odell.

Even in total destruction, the monastery on Monte Cassino had a towering nobility, but the Allies lost more than 45,000, killed or wounded. In addition, although the Germans also lost heavily, they successfully disengaged without being cut off following the American breakout from the Anzio beachhead.

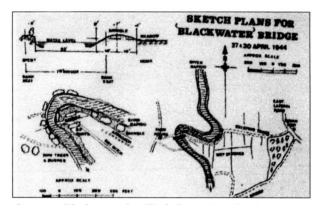

Operation Blackwater, *the Allied plan against Cassino.*

Charles lies in the shadow of Monte Cassino in the serene war cemetery, and he is commemorated on the Cassino Memorial, in the Stratford-upon-Avon Baptist Church, in the Garden of Remembrance in Old Town, and in the Memorial Library at King Edward VI School. Financed by the Italian State and reconsecrated in 1964 by Pope Paul VI, the monastery of Monte Cassino has been restored to its earlier beauty. All the archives were returned, including irreplaceable manuscripts and more than 1,400 codices that had been transferred, with great foresight, to the Vatican for safekeeping in December 1942.

> *The men I knew were young*
> *They'd always be young*
> *But we who are left*
> *Are left to be old.*
> Sapper, Royal Engineers, Cassino

Notes
1. A Sapper was a member of the Corps of Royal Engineers, the equivalent rank to a private soldier.

Chapter 42

JOHN PHILIP ORGAN

Warrant Officer, Pilot, 18 Squadron
22 May 1944

Dawn with its gradual bugles found them soaring,
And sunset made of earth a kindly toy
A.J.P. Herbert, *The Secret Battle*

In the rolling grasslands of the North Downs and set on two islands on the river Len, which flows through beds of water buttercups and marsh marigolds, Leeds Castle was a royal residence from 1278. Surrounded by parkland designed by Capability Brown, there are oaks and sweet chestnuts in the medieval deer park, with primroses, bluebells and woody nightshade, with gentle pasture fields beyond with clover and meadow vetchling. Jean Froissart described a visit there to Richard II in his *Chronicles*, and Elizabeth was imprisoned briefly in the castle during the reign of Mary I. The castle escaped destruction during the Civil War and passed to the Fairfax family. Revenue from the family estates in Virginia allowed for extensive repair in the early nineteenth century. When the castle was bought by Olive, Lady Baillie, in 1926, she initiated major restoration by craftsmen from France, Italy and Britain. In March 1934, her son Gawaine was born, and when he was four years old, Philip Organ was engaged as his nursery footman, a position held until 1940, when Philip joined an RAF Operational Training Unit.

Philip had entered the Preparatory School of King Edward VI at the age of six in January 1927 (Richard Spender was also a pupil at the time) and moved to the Grammar School in May 1928, remaining there until he was ten, when he became a boarder at Addington School in Berkshire. His sister remembers him as a lively, fair-haired boy, with very blue eyes.

Following training he was ordered to 18 Squadron, in time for its return to Britain following withdrawal from France and reassignment to anti-shipping duties in Blenheims. This included attacks on German invasion barges in French ports and later installations in Germany. With the Blenheim Mk V the squadron was transferred to Malta in late 1941, where they were engaged in raids against German and Italian shipping principally engaged in supplying the Axis forces in North Africa. Italy had lost 74 per cent of her shipping space employed on the African

Philip Organ.

campaign routes, and the tonnage left was only 65,000 tons. German shipments to North Africa had suffered heavy losses of ships, materials and men. As a result, Hitler ordered U-boats into the Mediterranean, and established the Luftwaffe in Sicily for the express purpose of neutralizing Malta. The endless air raids on Malta made it the most frequently bombed place of the whole war. No. 18 Squadron lost a number of aircraft in battles with Me 109s and were withdrawn to Britain to be reformed with new aircraft. This presented Philip with home leave, his last, and he enjoyed meeting those school friends that were not overseas in the services themselves.

Moving to North Africa in November 1942, the squadron accompanied the Allied armies as they advanced during the Western Desert Campaign, and supported the invasion of Sicily. It was re-equipped with the Douglas A-20 'Havoc' bomber – known among British and Commonwealth aircrew as 'Boston' – which distinguished itself as a dependable combat aircraft with speed and manoeuvrability. Crews liked the Boston as a light bomber and night fighter. The RAF had helped to cripple the Axis forces in North Africa and also took their toll of German and Italian shipping and aircraft during the fighting in Sicily.

With the successful invasion of Italy, Philip, now a warrant officer, flew first from Brindisi, then Foggia and, after February 1944, from Marcianise, north of Naples. Operations were against German communications in Italy and across the Adriatic in the Balkans. It was during of one of the missions against coastal shipping that Philip's Douglas Boston was lost without trace.

Outside the main entrance to Valletta in Malta is the memorial to the airmen of the Commonwealth who have no known grave. Standing 50 feet high and surmounted by a golden eagle, and made of travertine marble from the Tivoli area near Rome, the memorial has nineteen panels with the names of the 2,301 men who died.

Philip is also commemorated in the Garden of Remembrance in Old Town, and in the Memorial Library in King Edward VI School.

> *A place of sleep and warmth to eke their joy,*
> *And bring them love's release from their exploring.*
> A.J.P. Herbert

Notes
1. At Leeds Castle during the war, Lady Baillie hosted as part of their recovery Commonwealth airmen who had been burned in combat.
2. Gawaine Baillie succeeded to the family title in 1947, becoming 7th Baronet of Polkemmet, Linlithgowshire, and owned the estate surrounding Leeds Castle. Between 1956 and 1967 he enjoyed a successful career in motor racing. By the time of his death in 2003 he had assembled one of the greatest collections of postage stamps from Great Britain and the British Empire. Nine-tenths of the collection was sold at Sotheby's for £15 million.

Chapter 43

NORMAN ROLAND VICTOR WATSON

Captain, 2nd Battalion, Royal Ulster Rifles
30 June 1944

*On Normandy's green fields
where the hedgerows still run
and the sands on the beaches
lie quiet as air*
John Kent, *Yes, We Remember*

When Norman Watson was born in 1921 he was given the additional names of Roland Victor in memory of an uncle who had served with the East Surrey Regiment and been killed during the Second Battle of Arras in September 1918. The eldest of four brothers, who were all pupils at King Edward VI School, Norman participated fully in the life of the school, playing in the same 1st XV as Rogers Miller, Alan Woodward and James Overbury, earning his 2nd XV colours, becoming a prefect and Captain of De La Warr House. Joining the National Farmers' Union Mutual Insurance Society he maintained connection with the school by playing for the Old Edwardians XV. In 1939 he enlisted into the Territorial Army shortly before the outbreak of war, and in 1940 joined the Royal Warwickshire Regiment. Following attendance at an Officer Cadet Training School he was drafted into 2nd Battalion, The Royal Ulster Rifles, and commissioned as a captain.

Norman Watson.

First as a platoon commander in A Company, he spent several months as Battalion Intelligence Officer before the regiment moved to Hawick in the Scottish Borders when he

2nd Battalion Royal Ulster Rifles.

became Second-in-Command of C Company. His thoroughness and sense of responsibility was considered of great assistance in the administration of the company. He played full-back for the battalion XV, and encouraged others with his enthusiasm as the battalion swimming and cross-country officer. Those months in Hawick were enjoyable, and he earned a reputation for his team spirit and good humour, with a high devotion to duty.

By 1944 he was on the staff at Brigade Headquarters and Aide-de-Camp to Major General James Steele, when 2nd Battalion moved to Droxford, near Portsmouth, in preparation for the D-Day landings. Every wood in the South of England concealed an army unit, and the 2nd Battalion embarked on craft and sailed to Littlehampton for an 'exercise in the Channel that was heavily supported by the Royal Navy and Royal Air Force'. Morale was high, and on 22 May, King George VI inspected the brigade, the last big parade before 6 June. On 1 June he wrote to his brother Bryan: 'Life here is not too bad although I shall be jolly glad to get started – we'll soon finish this job off.'

Operation *Jubilee* in August 1942, which had been ill-conceived and had cost Robert Parks-Smith his life, taught the Allies that a combined assault on German-occupied Europe had to be comprehensively planned in every aspect of the operation. Following the Dieppe Raid, a German commander observed that it would be an error to believe that the enemy would mount the next operation in the same manner. 'Next time he will do things differently.'

Planning began in early 1943 for the next large-scale invasion of Europe, and although the Pas de Calais was the most obvious choice, it was also the most heavily defended section of Hitler's Atlantic Wall. It also had high cliffs, and narrow beaches with restricted exits. Normandy was chosen because it had none of these drawbacks, being lesser fortified and with wide beaches that were sheltered from the prevailing winds.

The invasion on 6 June 1944 took place along a 50-mile stretch of the Normandy coast divided into five landings on the beaches, called Utah, Omaha, Gold, Juno and Sword. During the night, airborne troops of the 6th Airborne Division, commanded by an Old Boy of King Edward VI School, Major General Richard Gale, had landed inland behind the German positions.

The 2nd Battalion Royal Ulster Rifles were part of the 9th Infantry Brigade 3rd Infantry Division, which came ashore on Sword Beach. Awaiting the assault along the shoreline, the German defenders braced for action. As the day progressed they had little knowledge of what was going on around them and, for all their elaborate fixed positions, in the days that followed the invasion, they enjoyed only a slight advantage fighting in the flat and open terrain. They were widely dispersed, the attackers sharply concentrated.

The most important objective and the key to the whole invasion had been given to 3rd Infantry Division – the capture of Caen, which dominated a plateau about 7 miles from the landing point, and which would give access to good tank country all the way to Paris. On 7 June they met an enemy they learned to fear: the SS Hitlerjugend Panzer Division.

Normandy was a mixture of cornfields and small fields with sunken lanes and high dense hedges, undulating and twisting dusty roads, and trees with great cover for the Germans. Every yard had to be fought for, and the country from the beachhead inland became a veritable killing ground.

After three weeks of heavy fighting, Norman reached Cambes-en-Plaine, where the battalion made its headquarters in the

Memorial at Cambes-en-Plaine.

chateau. Unfortunately, the Germans had the chateau and the area of the battalion's HQ exactly in range of their guns, and were able to target anyone who showed themselves out of a slit trench. During an exchange of fire on 30 June, Norman was hit by a stray shell and killed. Buried at first in the slit trench where he died, Norman was later buried in La Delivrande War Cemetery at Douvres, 7 miles north of Caen. His commanding officer wrote of the great loss to the whole battalion, and a friend remembered his frank and unassuming character, which 'won him many friends who were the richer for his companionship, and to whom his loss will be sad indeed.'

Norman Watson is commemorated on the memorial at Cambes-en-Plaine, on the Alveston War Memorial, on the Roll of Honour of the Royal Ulster Rifles, and in the Memorial Library at King Edward VI School.

And each waning day,
as the sea mourns alone,
the soft sound of Taps
flows over the fields
John Kent, *Yes, We Remember*

Notes
1. In 1934, Norman was presented with a Parker fountain pen by his English master, James Ferguson, for his excellence in handwriting. Amongst his personal possessions returned to his parents following his death in Normandy, the pen was presented to the school by his brother Bryan in 2005 and is displayed in the Archive in the Memorial Library.

Chapter 44

CYRIL BROOKING THORNTON MBE

Flight Lieutenant, Pilot, 501 Squadron
21 August 1944

All that kills abundant living,
Let it from the earth be banned:
Pride of status, race or schooling,
Dogmas that obscure our plan.
In our common quest for justice
May we hallow life's brief span.
From the Kreuzkirche, in Dresden

August 1944, and in the evening glow, the bats and swallows were flying around the tall, dark trees. The swallows were making their last, almost feverish, journeys through the radiance of the evening air. The bats came suddenly from the shadows of the trees into the bright, clear light of the sundown glow with sharp definition, to vanish as suddenly into the dusk of trees and hedges.

A new sound had appeared in the skies of Southern England during the summer – a distinctive noise of a pulse jet engine that cut out at a predetermined mileage and delivered a tonne of high explosives. The silence between the engine stopping and the explosion was as if everyone was holding their breath. The horses would stop and keep their feet still. The bakers and milkmen would stop their rumbling carts. What little traffic there was would sometimes stop, just waiting. Launched from sites in the Pas de Calais, they were the last great challenge of the Second World War that the people had to face. Called 'Vergeltungswaffen', the weapon of revenge for the relentless bombing of German cities, they were pilotless and flew low at 350mph. The distinctive noise betrayed their presence, the following silence warned of danger. Becoming known as V-weapons, the public would call them 'doodlebugs', 'buzz bombs' or 'flying bombs'.

Anti-aircraft batteries were unable to hit them because they flew too low, but some exploded on the barrage balloons over the city. Many were shot down by resolute pilots of Spitfires, Typhoons or Tempest Mk 5s of 501 Squadron, who dived on them from a height in order to get sufficient speed to shoot from behind. The Tempest was the fastest low-medium altitude fighter and became the mainstay against the V-weapon. The preferred method was for the pilot to fly alongside the 'bomb' and position his wing directly above its wing in order to disrupt the airflow, and cause it to veer into a dive. The great risk was always that a pilot would be killed by the blast of the exploding flying bomb, and this is what happened to Flight Lieutenant Cyril Thomas.

Joining 501 Squadron from OTU in 1939 after he had left school, where he had boarded in School House, Cyril had been a fervent sportsman as a member of both the 1st XV and 1st IX teams. An enthusiastic captain of De La Warr House, he had also made notable appearances for the Shakespeare Society's productions of *Richard II* and *The Two Gentlemen of Verona.*

The squadron was ordered to France on 10 May 1940 and was involved in the weeks of the Battle of France, stationed at Bethenville, Anglur and Le Mans, and later in the subsequent evacuation of British troops. Returning to England on 20 June, they reorganized at RAF Croydon before moving to RAF Middle Wallop – where Rogers Miller was with 609 Squadron – and then to RAF Gravesend, where they saw action during the Battle of Britain.

Transferring to RAF Kenley, near Croydon, the squadron had a brief flirtation with night fighting in Hurricanes before being equipped with Spitfires in April 1941. They remained at Kenley until moving to Ballyhalbert in County Down, Northern Ireland, for six months, and then to RAF Manston in Kent, where the squadron formed part of the Air Defence of Great Britain flying the Tempest Mk V.

In the main, the operations carried out were high-altitude fighter sweeps, anti-shipping reconnaissance, and offensive operations known as 'Rangers', which were long-range sorties inside enemy territory specifically to attack German vehicles.

In November 1943, a Mosquito carrying full operational equipment and long-range petrol tanks, crashed while taking off from RAF Manston and immediately burst into flames. Soon there were more explosions as fuel tanks, cannon shells and Verey cartridges ignited. Blazing wreckage was flung in all directions. One of the first to arrive on the scene of the accident, Cyril found that the Mosquito's navigator had been thrown clear. Making him comfortable, he organized the medical party and supervised his removal to an ambulance. *The London Gazette* of 14 March 1944 described:

> Then, with complete disregard of his own safety, this officer made straight for the main area of the crash which was surrounded by barbed wire, and saw the pilot of the aircraft was lying beside an engine with his clothing on fire. Flying Officer Thornton went

through the wire into the middle of the wreckage to reach the pilot, and, in spite of the great danger he was in, put out the flames on the pilot's clothing, and removed his parachute. With assistance he then carried the pilot to an ambulance. Unfortunately, both the rescued airmen died later but had it not been for the prompt and gallant action of Flying Officer Thornton, who sustained burns to both hands, neither would have been rescued alive.

Gazetted for Brave Conduct, Cyril was awarded the Member of the Order of the British Empire (MBE).

At the beginning of the flying bomb attacks, Cyril, now Flight Lieutenant, was covering Channel convoys and sweeps over Northern France following the D-Day landings. Defence units had been trying out various ways of knocking out the 'bombs', and 501 Squadron was given the task of eliminating them before they reached London. The squadron had considerable success, and Cyril recorded nine 'kills', often nonchalantly tipping the wing of the flying bomb and sending it crashing into the Kent countryside. He did this once too often, and on 21 August,

Cyril's Tempest challenges a V1.

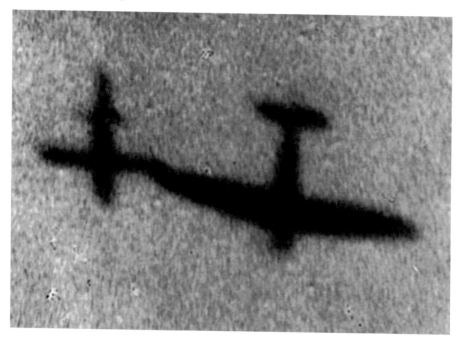

a flying bomb exploded on contact and Cyril's Tempest was destroyed by the blast. He is commemorated on the memorial in Margate Cemetery, in the RAF Manston History Museum, and in the Memorial Library at King Edward VI School.

Some day we will know, where the pilot's go
When their work on earth is through.
Where the air is clear, and the engines gleam,
And the skies are always blue.
Unknown author, pilot's poem

Margate Cross of Honour.

Notes
1. De La Warr House was named after Charles Richard Sackville West, 6th Earl De La Warr, who was High Steward of Stratford-upon-Avon in 1853.

Chapter 45

GEOFFREY CROSS
Flight Officer, 185 Squadron
23 August 1944

Flight is freedom in its purest form,
To dance with the clouds which follow a storm;
To roll and glide, to wheel and spin,
To feel the joy that swells within.
Gary Claude Stoker, *Impressions of a Pilot*

Canada was considered ideal as a location for the British Commonwealth Air Training Plan, set up in 1940 as a joint programme created by the United Kingdom, Canada, Australia and New Zealand for military aircrew training. In time, nearly half the aircrew that served in their forces were trained in Canada, with its wide open spaces, industrial facilities for production of aircraft, and supplies of fuel. Several boys from King Edward VI School were trained in Canada, and some, to their initial frustration, were to remain there as instructors and never see action. But they were young, and they took their fortunes lightly. Most were rather conscientious boys striving to fulfil that eternal maxim that achievement must be apparently effortless, and above all they must not seem to care. Yet when the war ended, one or two experienced feelings of guilt, that they had remained safe in Canada, had survived, whilst their friends had died. Eventually, of course, these feelings eased.

One pilot trained in Canada was Geoffrey Cross. A particularly striking academic, he had achieved a great deal while at school – Captain of De La Warr House, being awarded his 1st XV colours, a popular prefect, and had performed with his friend Richard Spender in the Dramatic Society productions of *Vice Versa* and *The Rehearsal*. He went to Birmingham University, gaining his International BSc as a research chemist under Herbert Muggleton Stanley, himself an Old Boy of King Edward VI School, who had won

Geoffrey Cross in the 1st XV.

174

the Shakespeare Exhibition to Birmingham in 1919, and had established a highly motivated and fully integrated research department.

As sadly happened to Patrick Overton while training in the United States in 1942, in Canada, low flying was the most significant cause of accidents and fatalities, often explained as the result of pilots' skill not matching their daring. Rather, the result of a few exuberant students pushing their luck. Happily this was not the case with Geoffrey Cross, who achieved his wings as a pilot and returned to England in 1942 to join 185 Squadron, in time to fly Spitfires from Takali and Hal Far for the battles over Malta.

Strategically, Malta was in a vital position virtually at the centre of the Mediterranean, 57 miles south of Sicily, 179 miles north of Africa, with Gibraltar 1,133 miles to the west and Syria 1,205 miles to the east. A British possession with three airfields and a naval dockyard, it was an ideal launching post for

Geoffrey Cross.

air and sea strikes against ships bound for North Africa. When war began, Malta's defences were almost non-existent, and all sides recognized the importance of the island in controlling the Mediterranean.

When they first arrived in Malta in 1941, the squadron's Hurricanes had been outclassed by the new German Me 109 and the Italian Macchi C202, suffering very high losses, and severely weakening the island's offensive naval and air capabilities. With their advantage in the air, the Germans enjoyed considerable success with mine-laying, which caused heavy losses of Allied submarines. This superiority also allowed for successful transport of German and Italian supplies to North Africa.

The arrival of Spitfires at the end of 1942 restored the balance, and allowed the squadrons on Malta to go onto the offensive. The Hurricanes could now concentrate on the enemy bombers at lower heights, and the Spitfires dealt with those aircraft at higher levels. At sea by May 1943, over 230 German and Italian ships had been sunk, with the loss of a large percentage of fuel and supplies badly needed by the Afrika Korps.

During this period also, Geoffrey and other members of 185 Squadron took part in sweeps over Sicily, and by July 1943 he was involved in the air support during the invasion of Sicily until victory at Messina in August. During the invasion of Italy, the squadron was based at Grottaglie on the Salento peninsula, which divides the Adriatic Sea from the Ionian Sea, in the province of Taranto in Southern Italy. Grottaglie was used by the United States Army Air Force for its strategic bombing campaign against Germany and for supporting ground forces during the Italian campaign.

In August 1944, the squadron transferred to Perugia in Umbria, in central Italy, near the Tiber River. It had been the home of Pietro Vannucci, called Perugino, who worked in Rome and Florence during the Renaissance, and was the teacher of Raphael. From here the squadron was engaged in operations, and it is believed that flying Spitfire Mk IX MA249, Geoffrey was wounded by fire from a Junkers Ju 88 and died days later on 23 August. He was buried in the Ancona War Cemetery, which overlooks the Adriatic Sea. He is commemorated in the Garden of Remembrance in Old Town, Stratford-upon-Avon and in the Memorial Library at King Edward VI School.

And most of them are gone, the gay, the bright ones,
Whose laughter was too spiral for the earth
A.J.P. Herbert

Notes

1. Herbert Muggleton Stanley was a very eminent chemist and the guiding genius behind the invention and development of novel chemical processes, and hailed as one of the makers of the modern world. He was elected a Fellow of the Royal Society in 1966.

Chapter 46

THE REVEREND
CANON CLIFFORD JOHN COHU
Rector of St Saviour's Church, Jersey
20 September 1944

'Don't worry, God's on my side!'
Clifford Cohu, 1942

Closer to Normandy than to Britain, the Channel Islands were occupied from 30 June 1940 until their liberation on 9 May 1945. The Germans quickly moved in infantry, and established both communication centres and anti-aircraft defences. Living on Jersey at the time of occupation was Clifford Cohu, who was the popular acting rector (Ministre Desservant) of St Saviour's Church in St Helier. Born on Guernsey, where he attended Elizabeth College, he moved to Yorkshire when his father, the Reverend Jean Rougier Cohu, became headmaster of Richmond School. As a school inspector, his father visited King Edward VI School, and was so impressed that he arranged for his son to become a boarder in School House between 1897 and 1900. Clifford excelled in Divinity, English Grammar, Latin, Greek and French. In a ceremony never performed before in its 800-year history, he was confirmed by the Bishop of Worcester in December 1898 in the Guild Chapel. Following studies at Keble College, Oxford, he was ordained in 1907 and served as a curate in Ripon in North Yorkshire, and then in Hawarden, on the Welsh border, where he married, but lost twin children who died in infancy.

Between 1912 and 1934, he was a military chaplain in India, first at Banares, then later at Lucknow, before being appointed as Canon of Allahabad Cathedral and given the rank of colonel in the military chaplaincy. A member of the Indian Ecclesiastical Establishment, he was highly regarded for his honesty and chivalry, which earned him the affection of the local Indians, who called him 'pukka sahib'. Years later, a friend was to observe that 'twenty-three years in India had a profound influence on the highly sensitive man.'

During his journey home to England, he was appointed briefly to the Anglican Church in Palermo, before settling happily on Jersey in 1937. When the position of Rector of St Saviour's Church in St Helier became vacant, Clifford was appointed as Ministre Desservant and enjoyed widespread popularity. These were happy years for him.

Following their lightning thrust through France, the Germans were poised to occupy the Channel Islands off the north-west coast of France. Unable to defend them, the British Government offered to evacuate the people, and several thousand escaped before the Germans arrived on 30 June. The islands' own authority kept the running of affairs – approved by the German Commandant – and advised passive co-operation, but a number of provocative incidents frequently occurred. Rationing, curfews, deportations, and the supervision of fishing vessels were all strictly supervised.

Cohu identity card.

In June 1942, the German authorities on the Channel Islands, aware that many people were still able to listen to the news from the BBC, placed a ban on the possession of radio sets and ordered that all were to be confiscated. A great number were handed in but many were not. In addition, all kinds of crystal sets were made and became virtually undetectable. The German authorities became nervous about this popular act of disobedience. The order was difficult to enforce, and as flouting it was looked upon by the Germans as an act of defiance, a second, more draconian, order was displayed in December, declaring that those caught listening to the BBC broadcasts would be imprisoned.

A group at St Saviour's had an illegal radio. It belonged to a farm labourer, and another, a gardener, was responsible for digging it up and reburying it afterwards. The gravedigger typed out the information, and Clifford passed on the details as he performed his chaplaincy duties at the General Hospital, often declaring, 'Wonderful news today!' He also cycled along the Parade in St Helier shouting the news. Once warned by a nurse at the hospital, Cohu replied: 'Don't worry. God's on my side!' On another occasion, deliberately disobeying another restriction, he invited his congregation to sing *God Save the King*, which they did at the top of their voices.

Such behaviour was rather innocuous, but it landed him at the top of the Germans' list of undesirables, and when the secret police found the radio, he was arrested on 12 March 1943, taken to their headquarters at Havre des Pas, and his trial took place a month later. The outcome was clear from the start, as the Germans were determined to rid Jersey of Cohu, but the sentence, considering his age, was certainly disproportionately harsh in contrast with others for the same offence.

Local opinion believed that 'his chief fault in the eyes of the Germans was that he tried to keep up other people's spirits.' He was a man, a friend later remembered, who persistently refused to be caught by the cheap simplicity of logic that ignores half of human nature. 'He would not purchase emphasis at the cost of ignoring obvious facts. If life is one-sided, as it certainly is, then faith that is one-sided stands convicted of inadequacy: he knew that the solution of a complicated problem cannot but be complicated itself.'

Clifford was sentenced to eighteen months' imprisonment for 'failing to surrender leaflets and disseminating anti-German news'. After three months in Gloucester Street Prison, where life was not harsh, Clifford was deported first to Fort d'Hauteville, near Dijon, and then to Saarbrücken in Germany. Suffering extreme cold and hunger, he worked nine hours each day putting hooks into cardboard. In January 1944 he was transferred to the prison at Frankfurt-Preungesheim, where he was kept in solitary confinement. Receiving minimal rations his weight dropped dramatically in conditions where dysentery was rampant. In August he was moved again, this time to Spergau Concentration Camp, near Leipzig, where the exhausted Canon Cohu was put to work digging. Far too weak for the task, he was singled out, as *'der Englischen'*, by the SS guards for savage daily beatings.

So brutally beaten on 17 September, he was left on the straw floor of a paper tent. Three days later, he died. After his death a survivor told that a small bible was found tightly pressed against his heart, which Clifford had somehow managed to conceal in spite of numerous body searches. It was the last act of defiance by an extraordinary man, whose body had been abused and broken, but whose faith had remained indomitable. Although some doubt remains, it is likely that Clifford's body was taken for cremation at Halle.

An appreciation of Canon Cohu appeared in the *Jersey Evening Post* on 29 September 1945, and a two-part account of his life was published in the *Sunday Island Times* in March 1994. 'He was the nicest man you could ever hope to meet,'

Occupation Tapestry.

a friend recalled, 'but I wince now when I remember him coming down St Saviour's Hill on his bicycle, and calling out to me the latest BBC news at the top of his voice.' Clifford is commemorated on a plaque in St Saviour's Church in St Helier, on the Jersey War Memorial, and on the Occupation Tapestry, which was produced by more than 300 islanders and is displayed in the Maritime Museum in St Helier. He is also commemorated in the Memorial Library at King Edward VI School, and a portrait of Canon Clifford Cohu by Edmund Blampied hangs in the Jersey General Hospital.

> *O Jesus, I have promised*
> *To serve Thee to the end;*
> *Be Thou forever near me,*
> *My Master and my Friend.*
> John E. Bode, Hymns Ancient and Modern

Notes
1. The farmer, the gardener and the gravedigger all perished in German concentration camps.

Chapter 47

NORMAN FREDERICK PARKES
Sergeant, Royal Army Pay Corps
8 January 1945

He only lived but till he was a man,
The which no sooner had his prowess confirmed
William Shakespeare, *Macbeth*, Act 5 Scene 11

Norman Parkes.

Crossing the river Alne, the tree-lined High Street in Henley-in-Arden was the main road between Stratford-upon-Avon and Birmingham. Approaching the centre of the town and on the right-hand side of the High Street was a house with an attractive bow window. This was the stationer's shop of Herbert Parkes, his wife Rose and their three children, George, Norman and Beatrice. Herbert's father George had been a trustee elected by the Parish Council, and in 1917 had challenged the ancient 'Lord's Waste' by placing a bow window to his house and therefore was 'assessed to pay 6d a year'. This old law referred to the land between the pavement and the front of a property on the High Street. The family were Baptists. Beatrice played the organ at their church in Henley-in-Arden, and Herbert played the organ at the Baptist church in Tanworth-in-Arden. He travelled there on his motorcycle, and one evening in 1938, he was killed skidding on an icy road.

Norman had attended King Edward VI School between January 1934 and December 1935, in the same form group as James Overbury and the same year as Norman Watson. Tall, fair-haired and wearing glasses, Norman's great hobby was railways, similar to the one on which he travelled each day to school. He had always been good with figures, and on leaving school at sixteen he was employed in the office of a local chartered accountant.

He enlisted in the local Territorial Army unit in 1939, and then, on 2 September 1940, was posted to the headquarters of Western Command in Chester. Like his brother and sister, Norman suffered from chest problems and was not strong, but his health classification was Grade III (B5) and he became a private in the Royal

181

Army Pay Corps (RAPC). After successfully passing a series of instruction classes, he was attached to the office of the Commander Royal Engineers (CRE), Central Midlands Area (Worcestershire, Warwickshire and Herefordshire), in St John's House, Coten End in Warwick. Norman's responsibilities in the RAPC office were numerous and diverse, and would place him, on one occasion, on the periphery of one of the significant events of the war.

The 3,000 men of the Czech Brigade arrived in Leamington Spa on a frosty day in October 1940. Their headquarters was established in a large Victorian villa in the centre of the town, while the various units of the brigade were dispersed to military installations and to country houses in the area that had been requisitioned – Moreton Paddox, Moreton Morrell, Wellesbourne and Kineton. They had arrived in Britain three months earlier quite disillusioned and demoralized, after being rushed into battle in May 1940. When France surrendered, the Czechs were abandoned and only rescued at the last minute. Not a crack unit like the Cossack Guard of Imperial Russia, they were, on the whole, well educated men who had sacrificed everything for their country, had a bitter hatred of the Germans, and wanted to create a better society in Czechoslovakia when the war was over. As the winter turned to spring, with the cherry trees blossoming along the streets of Leamington, a plan was developed for spectacular resistance against the German occupation of Czechoslovakia. Named Operation *Anthropoid,* the target was Reinhard Heydrich, the brutal Reichsprotektor of Bohemia and Moravia.

Recruitment of volunteers for 'Special Operations' began at Leamington Spa in the spring of 1941, and they arrived at special Secret Training Schools (STS) of the Special Operations Executive (SOE). A group of these trained volunteers parachuted into Czechoslovakia in December 1941, and fatally wounded Heydrich in Prague on 27 May 1942. Following his death and those of all the Czech parachutists, the German reprisals included the execution of more than 5,000 Czech civilians and the complete destruction of the village of Lidice.

The Royal Army Pay Corps was also responsible for paying those involved in the Western Command Droitwich to Watling Street Stop Line. The objective was to divide England into several 'small fields' surrounded by a 'hedge' of anti-tank obstacles using natural obstacles where possible. The Droitwich Stop Line started from the river Severn at Upper Arley, north of Bewdley, proceeded overland to the river Avon at Binton and then along the river Avon to Stratford-upon-Avon. It then followed the river Avon to Warwick and Leamington Spa, ran along the London, Midland and Scottish Railway line to Rugby and then the river Swift to Watling Street at the boundary of the Western and Northern Commands. A Southern Command memorandum explained that 'should airborne attacks break into the enclosures the policy will be to close the gate by blocking the crossing over the obstacle and let in the "dogs" in the shape of armoured formations, or other troops, to "round up the cattle".' The anti-tank islands were at Redditch,

Henley-in-Arden, Kidderminster, Stratford-upon-Avon, Warwick/Leamington Spa, Northampton, Kettering and Worcester.

Towards the end of 1942, the 1st Belgian Independent Infantry Brigade headquarters and training units, commanded by Major Jean-Baptiste Piron, were based at Kineton, south of Stratford-upon-Avon, and at Umberslade Park, by Tamworth-in-Arden, and with sub-units at Moreton Morrell and Walton Hall, near Wellesbourne. Their finances were administered from St John's House. Similarly when 2,000 Italian, then German, prisoners of war were kept in four permanent buildings at Cloisters Croft, off Lillington Avenue, in Leamington Spa.

Promoted to sergeant in 1944, during that year Norman's health began to deteriorate as the chest problem that had often brought concern became serious, so much so that on 20 November 1944 he was admitted to the Hertford Hill Sanatorium at Hatton. The King Edward VII Memorial Hospital was the central hospital for mentally ill patients, and the sanatorium for the treatment of tuberculosis was in a number of buildings apart from the main hospital building. Set in beautiful countryside, it was isolated because at the time both of these illnesses carried a degree of social stigma. Quickly his condition worsened, with a chronic infectious inflammation of the lungs. In the 1940s, the treatment was absolute rest, no movement except going to the toilet once a day, propped up by pillows and with no deep breathing. It was the life of a log. Over Christmas and New Year, Norman developed pulmonary tuberculosis and he died on 8 January 1945. He was twenty-five.

It was not known where Norman was buried. Researching his army life was a puzzle that turned into a mystery. In spite of his army records stating that he was in the Royal Army Pay Corps, the organization's record office has no record of him or of an office in Warwick, although the National Archives confirmed St John's House. Records held in Warwick state and list the gravesite number in which he was buried in the churchyard of St Nicholas's Church in Henley-in-

Hertford Hill Sanatorium, Hatton.

Arden. No such number is listed on the graveyard record. By tradition, Baptists were buried in the graveyard of a Baptist church, and the church that the family attended in Henley-in-Arden has only one grave inscribed to a member of the Parkes family, his grandfather, George. Several churchyards around the Henley and Tamworth-in-Arden area were searched, until a local historian, Dr Douglas Bridgewater, discovered his record of a conversation he had with Norman Welsh, one of the oldest inhabitants of Henley. He had been a friend and pallbearer when Norman was buried in an unmarked grave in the churchyard of the Baptist church in Henley.

Norman is, however, commemorated on the brass war memorial in St John's Church in Henley-in-Arden and in the Memorial Library at King Edward VI School.

your cause of sorrow
Must not be measured by his worth, for then
It hath no end.
William Shakespeare, *Macbeth*, Act 5 Scene 11

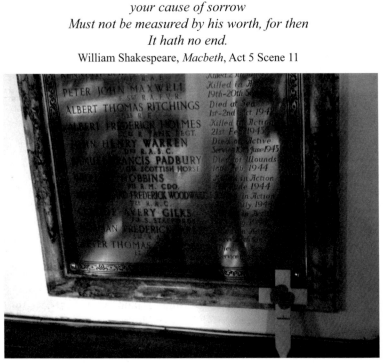

War memorial in Henley-in-Arden.

Notes
1. Surviving comrades of the parachutists who assassinated Heydrich erected a memorial fountain to their memory in 1968 in Jephson Gardens in Leamington Spa. On either side of the fountain they planted heather brought from Lidice.
2. St John's House today has displays of Warwickshire social history, and on the upper floor it houses the Museum of the Royal Regiment of Fusiliers (Royal Warwickshire).

Chapter 48

THOMAS CORBETT HIATT
Air Mechanic, 26 Squadron, South African Air Force
17 January 1945

No more by thee my steps shall be
For ever and for ever.
The Rivulet, traditional South African verse

Thomas Hiatt joined King Edward VI in mid-September 1921 once the harvest had been collected on his father's farm at Elmley Castle in Worcestershire. It was a pretty village of half-timbered cottages at the foot of Bredon Hill and 5 miles from Evesham. He had attended Greenhill School, a small private preparatory school in Evesham, and by the time he joined the school in Stratford-upon-Avon the family had moved to Manor Farm in Lower Quinton, in the beautiful countryside on the edge of the Cotswolds.

Leaving school in December 1929, he joined his father's farm. Opportunities to acquire land and farm in the British colonies had been a popular adventure since before the First World War and so, like David Crawford in John Buchan's novel *Prester John*, Thomas sailed to South Africa to make his fortune. In the 1930s, people in numbers travelled there from all walks of life, like moths to a flame, with visions of an enchanted and exotic life ostensibly offered by a city of gold. Johannesburg, with a sleazy glitz, hovered on the fringes of that world like a threatening and incomprehensible spectre of glamour and menace. Thomas's eyes and senses were beyond all that. He found a land of lush green grass with marigolds and arum lilies instead of daisies and buttercups. Thickets of tall trees dotted the hill slopes and patched the meadows as if some landscape gardener had been at work on them. Beyond, the glens fell steeply to the plains, which ran out in a faint haze to the horizon.

Thomas settled in the Bezuidenhout Valley, near Johannesburg, married and prospered during what for many in South Africa were the lean years of the worldwide Depression. When war broke out in September 1939, South Africa once again rallied to the British Empire's call to arms and, as in 1914, began to mobilize its forces. Although as a farmer he was in one of the reserved occupations, in time he nevertheless volunteered for the South African Air Force. After passing through its training unit, he became an air mechanic and was posted to 26 Squadron, which was based at Takorad in the Gold Coast, on the west coast of Africa. It was an important air base both as a staging point for British aircraft destined for Egypt and the Western Desert Campaign, and on the main line between Accra and Kumasi. Flying the Wellington Mk XI, 26 Squadron were engaged on anti-submarine convoy escort patrols over the South Atlantic, protecting the convoy route from the United States to the Middle East.

The Germans were always increasing the anti-aircraft armament of the U-boats, but in spite of several technological advances that caused temporary concern for the convoys, diving remained a U-boat's best chance of survival when attacked by the growing efficiency of Allied aircraft.

Ground crew.

Takoradi airbase.

Although by the end of 1944 the threat of the U-boats was really over, there was still the occasional threatening lone wolf that cruised the South Atlantic, and photo-reconnaissance was still needed in the gathering of intelligence. On one such operation, on 17 January 1945, Wellington Mk XI HZ 709 took off from Ikeja bound for Kano. It never arrived and the wreck was discovered some time later 4 miles from Ipapa. The four crew and five passengers all died. Except for two who were members of the Royal Air Force, all the others, including Thomas Hiatt, were members of the South African Air Force.

Thomas was buried in Yaba Cemetery on the outskirts of Lagos in Nigeria. He is commemorated on the War Memorial in Lower Quinton and in the Memorial Library at King Edward VI School.

> *My sword I give to him that shall succeed me in my pilgrimage,*
> *and my courage and skill to him that can get it.*
> *My marks and scars I carry with me.*
> John Bunyan, *The Pilgrim's Progress*
> (quoted at the end of *Mr Standfast* by John Buchan)

Lower Quinton war memorial.

Chapter 49

THOMAS ANTHONY TESTAR

Lieutenant, 27 Field Regiment, Royal Artillery
23 February 1945

On the road to Mandalay,
Where the old Flotilla lay,
With our sick beneath the awnings when we went to Mandalay!
Rudyard Kipling, *Mandalay*

By the beginning of 1945, with its skies virtually undefended and the Allied armies advancing towards the borders of Germany, the war in Europe appeared to be in the final stages. Meanwhile, in the jungles in Malaya the 'forgotten war' was being fought by the 'forgotten army' against a ferocious, tenacious and implacable enemy.

British staff officers had ridiculed the idea that the Japanese could be a serious fighting force, and jeered at the dwarf-like figures under their medieval helmets. Their weapons and aeroplanes, these officers declared, had been copied from the West, and would be no match for a modern European army. It was soon discovered that, man for man, the Japanese were the more formidable enemy. They had the advantages of fanatical bravery, the ability to march long distances at great speed, with minimal logistic support, and a belief called '*Seishin*' (strength of will), a spiritual essence that would overcome all obstacles. One of their Orders of the Day declared: 'Continue in the task until all your ammunition is expended. If your hands are broken, fight with your feet. If your hands and feet are broken, fight with your teeth. If there is no breath left in your body, fight with your spirit.'

Fighting in Burma was as terrible as fighting in the trenches in the First World War. The country was the size of France and Belgium combined, had two monsoon seasons, and from May to November was unbelievably hot and humid. Burma was a rich prize for the Japanese, partly for its oil, rubber and rice, but also as a stepping stone westwards into India.

The British campaign to push the Japanese out of Burma was the longest and bloodiest of the Second World War, and thousands of miles away from the battles in Western Europe, the soldiers believed that they had been forgotten.

One of those forgotten soldiers was Anthony (Tony) Testar. He had first joined the Territorial Army in Stratford-upon-Avon in April 1939, and later that year the Royal Engineers, and he was posted to 27 Field Regiment. Tony had arrived at King Edward VI School in 1928, and his friends included four boys, Arthur North, Philip Organ, Stanley Phillips and Leonard Merritt, whose stories appear in this book. He was an active and enthusiastic secretary of the Shakespeare Society, appearing as The Producer in a 1934 production of *The Rehearsal*, and in the same year played Panthino in *The Two Gentlemen of Verona* – a production that also included John Miller and Cyril Thornton. In 1935, he played Richard II 'with tragic intensity and fine feeling'; Standish Mottram played a Herald and

Tony Testar.

Thornton a 'vigorous' Aumerle. In his final year as a corporal in the Cadet Corps, he toured Mons, Namur, Marche-les-Dames and Waterloo.

Leaving school in the summer of 1935, he joined his father's business in Birmingham. Testar and Swain Limited were manufacturers of insecticide sprayers; very innovative ones, because their advertisements of the 1930s indicate a progressive diversity. He was there when war was declared in 1939, and he joined the Royal Engineers. The 27 Field Regiment was part of 1 Corps of the British Expeditionary Force (BEF) to Belgium in 1940 during the period of inaction that became known as the 'Phoney War'. 'Hitler,' declared the Prime Minister Neville Chamberlain, 'has missed the bus.' Caught by the Blitzkrieg as the German Panzers rolled through Holland and into France, the BEF retreated to the Channel coast. Evacuated from Dunkirk at the same time as William Lowth and the 124 Field Regiment, Tony and the rest of 27 Field Regiment returned to England for reorganization and rest. For the next two years they were engaged in various aspects of home defence, until in 1942 they received the order for transfer to the Far East to Headquarters Royal Artillery North West Army, India Command at Rawalpindi, where they joined 21 Field Battery.

India in the 1930s and early 1940s contained several revolutionary movements for independence from the British Raj (colonial rule), and although the resentment continued, Indians participated in the campaigns against both Germany and Japan. Its strategic position, production of armaments and armed forces helped decisively in the war in the Far East. Throughout the next two years, Testar's unit contributed to the defence of Eastern India as the Japanese launched a series of major offensives to drive through Burma and into India.

In March 1944, the Japanese, relying on mobility, infiltration and captured supplies, launched Operation *U-Go* to seize Assam and hopefully inspire a rising by the Indians against the British. A month earlier, an assault in the Imphal area was intended to divert British attention so that the momentum of the attack on Assam would be greater. Fighting was very fierce, and continued at Kohima and Imphal, with heavy casualties on both sides. The ability of a soldier to live and fight in the jungles of Burma required the highest level of physical toughness and

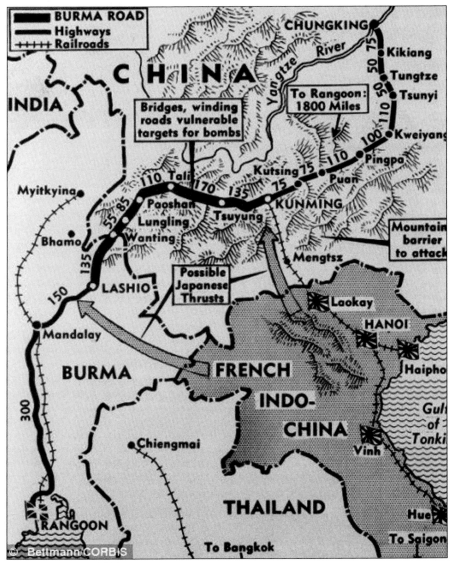

The war in Burma 1945.

initiative, to use ground and vegetation to the best advantage, to erect temporary shelters against tropical rain and to recognize and use the native foods. They hacked their way through green jungle, where the tops of the trees grew so close together that the sky became an emerald green patchwork flecked with blue. Green, red and yellow parrots squawked and chattering monkeys swung gleefully from branch to branch.

Unlike in earlier years, the arrival of the monsoon season did not bring an end to the campaigning, as the British harassed the Japanese supply lines and drove their lines towards the river Chindwin, west of Mandalay. By the end of 1944, the British forces were ready to advance on to the central plains of Burma. Using a combination of infantry and tanks, long columns moved southwards destroying Japanese resistance. Amphibious landings and bridgeheads were established over the rivers Chindwin and Irrawaddy, with the additional use of field batteries and machine-gun fire. The fighting was ferocious against a very determined enemy.

On 22 February, in support of an assault landing, Tony's unit was repeatedly attacked and he was severely wounded by shellfire. His courage and control of the battery gunfire was recognized as saving the lives of the infantry with him, and he was recommended for an immediate award of the Military Cross. In a letter to his wife, the Lieutenant Colonel of the 27 Field Regiment wrote that: 'the path down the hill to the hospital was difficult in the extreme, and caused a severe strain on the already seriously wounded men. I saw him in hospital and there was hope he would make it. He was operated on but most unfortunately he had not the strength left.' He died the following day, aged twenty-seven, and was buried in a quiet spot in a wood.

After the war, Tony Testar was buried in the Taukkyan War Cemetery, north of Rangoon (now Yangon) in Burma (now Myanmar). He is also commemorated in the Garden of Remembrance in Old Town, Stratford-upon-Avon and in the Memorial Library at King Edward VI School. On 11 November 1987, Elaine Testar and their son John visited Tony's grave during a pilgrimage to Burma.

> *On the road to Mandalay*
> *Where the flyin'-fishes play,*
> *An' the dawn comes up like thunder outer China 'cross the Bay!*
> Rudyard Kipling, *On the Road to Mandalay*

Notes
1. General Sir William Slim told the troops who fought in Burma: 'When you go home don't worry about what to tell your loved ones and friends about service in Asia. No one will know where you were, or where it is if you do. You are, and will remain "The Forgotten Army".'
2. In 2010, John Testar kindly presented copies of letters and photographs of his father's time in Burma to the KES Archive.

Chapter 50

SIDNEY CHARLES WILLIS
Flight Lieutenant, Royal Air Force Volunteer Reserve
3 March 1945

Only to fly through cloud, through storm, through night,
Unerring, and to keep their purpose bright,
Nor turn until their dreadful duty done
Westward they climb to race the awaked sun!
Bomber Command, Anon

With the German invasion of Yugoslavia in April 1941, the Allies soon recognized over the following months the potential of assisting the determined resistance by partisan groups. In spite of heavy commitments elsewhere, a number of planes from Egypt began dropping supplies for the groups of guerrilla fighters engaged in containing the occupation forces. Modest at first because of the heavy commitments elsewhere, the supply-dropping in time grew in size and significance and, by 1943, aircraft of the Strategic, Tactical and Coastal Air Forces were ranging along the Adriatic. Attacking ports, shipping, storage tanks, oil dumps, radio stations and gun emplacements, there was also emphasis placed on bombing marshalling yards and airfields. Supplies were dropped to partisans, wounded were evacuated, and air support helped in operations against German forces. This all led to the formation in June 1944 of the multinational Balkan Air Force (BAF) consisting of eight squadrons, with fifteen types of aircraft, and pilots and aircrew from eight nations. Based in Bari in Southern Italy, its commander was Air Vice-Marshall William Elliot, and it became a miniature General Headquarters. Elliot not only controlled the air forces but also co-ordinated all the other trans-Adriatic operations that included land forces. Of these, the most important were those in the Adriatic, the naval base at Taranto, military missions in Greece, Albania and Hungary, and those under Headquarters, Special Operations (Mediterranean). Up to October 1943, essential commitments in North Africa, the Sicilian Campaign, and the invasion of Italy had absorbed the whole of the Allied air striking force in the Mediterranean, but once firmly established on the mainland, units of the Tactical and Coastal Air Force began to fly over the Adriatic and Yugoslavia.

At one of the desks at Elliot's headquarters was Flight Lieutenant Sidney Willis, who had received his commission on 4 December 1943 into the General Duties Branch. His responsibilities included the conduct and supervision of all aspects of flying and engineering, and this included armament, wireless and photography as well as staff and administrative duties.

From Bari came the air support for SOE operations across the Adriatic and in the Aegean and Ionian seas. The BAF supported the operations of the Partisans led by Josip Tito against the German forces in Yugoslavia. These patriots waged guerrilla warfare and there were savage German reprisals. The Partisans suffered from damp, cold, lice, scurvy, hunger and thirst; medical supplies were scarce, and they carried their wounded with them.

One of Sidney Willis's friends at King Edward VI School, which he attended between 1925 and 1930, was fellow boarder Henry Peuleve, who became one of the most remarkable members of the French section of SOE. He had a close friendship with the secret agent Violette Szabo, and was one of the only agents to survive brutal treatment in Buchenwald concentration camp.

Bari Military Cemetery.

By the end of 1944 and into early 1945, Elliot's headquarters were hurling BAF heavy bomber night raids against retreating Germans in the Balkans. During the day with clear skies and sunshine lighting up the snow-covered countryside, Spitfires and rocket-firing Hurricanes ranged over German troop concentrations and rolling stock on the battlefield. Next came attacks on railways, road transport, bridges, viaducts and marshalling yards at Sofia, giving the retreating Germans no respite. By February, Willis's office was sending bombers to the marshalling yards and communication centres in Linz and Vienna, as well as the railway communications in Northern Yugoslavia, Hungary and Southern Germany.

Some time at the end of February, Sidney was involved in a flying accident, the details of which are not known, and he was moved to the 98th General Hospital in Bari, where he died of his injuries on 3 March. He was buried in the Bari Military Cemetery, and his headstone reads: 'Remembered with Honour'. On 1 January 1946, Sidney was Mentioned in Dispatches 'in recognition of his duties with the Balkans Air Force and with General Headquarters'. He is commemorated in the Memorial Library at King Edward VI School.

> *It's a lovely day tomorrow*
> *Tomorrow is a lovely day,*
> *Come and feast your tear dimmed eyes*
> *On tomorrow's clear blue skies.*
> Irving Berlin, *Tomorrow is a Lovely Day*

Notes

1. Henry Peuleve's life story is told in *Spirit of Resistance*, by Nigel Perrin.
2. The force under Elliot's command included British, South African, Italian, Greek, and Yugoslav; for the supply-dropping operations, American, Polish and Russian. The aircraft were Spitfires, Mustangs, Hurricanes, Beaufighters, Lysanders, Halifaxes, Baltimores, Dakotas, Liberators, Macchis, Fortresses, Marauders, Savoia-Machetti 82s, Cant 1007s, and Airacobras.

Chapter 51

ARTHUR JOHN AUST
Flying Officer, 68 Squadron
4 March 1945

they lived with us; we loved them;
We knew their tricks of gesture; how they smiled;
What foods and books they liked; but not the wild
Meridians of the heart that fired and proved them.
A.J.P. Herbert

'We live by death's negligence,' wrote Flying Officer James Farrar, who was killed on the night of 25 July 1944 while on patrol in a Mosquito trying to intercept a V1 flying bomb. He was a member of 68 Squadron, which had been established at RAF Catterick in 1941 as a defensive night fighter squadron equipped with the Bristol Blenheim and later the Bristol Beaufighter. The squadron moved first to High Ercall in Shropshire for the defence of the Midlands, and then to RAF Coltishall in Norfolk.

In June 1944, 68 Squadron converted to the de Havilland DH98 Mosquito, a multi-role combat aircraft nicknamed the 'Wooden Wonder'. Conceived as an unarmed fast bomber, it was adapted to several versatile roles including low-to-medium altitude daytime tactical bombing, plus as support 'to seek and destroy' enemy fighters in the air and on the ground (called 'Ranger ops'). It was also a high-altitude night bomber, pathfinder, day or night fighter, fighter-bomber and fast photo-reconnaissance aircraft. The Mosquito units supported strategic night fighter defence forces as well as successfully conducting night fighter sweeps as protection for Bomber Command's heavy raids over Occupied Europe and Germany. The Mosquito increased German night fighter losses so significantly that Reichsmarshall Hermann Goering, Commander-in-Chief of the Luftwaffe, ruefully declared: 'It makes me furious when I see the Mosquito. The British, who can afford aluminium better than we can, knock together a beautiful wooden aircraft that every piano factory over there is building.'

Arthur Aust was a member of 68 Squadron. He had enlisted in the Royal Air Force in 1935, and shortly following the declaration of war in September 1939, he flew as a pilot in France until June 1940. Subsequently posted to North Africa,

196

he was involved in the campaigns against the Italian and German air forces, was Mentioned in Dispatches and awarded the Africa Star. Returning to England in 1943, he was based at RAF Castle Camps on the Cambridgeshire/Essex border, some 70 flight miles from Coltishall, and was engaged on night fighter defence and Ranger operations, plus attacking specific European road and rail targets at night.

An enthusiastic cricketer who had played for the Alscot Park XI near Preston-on-Stour, he had enjoyed his sport at school between 1928 and 1933, bowling for the 2nd XI and playing rugby with the 2nd XV. On leaving school he joined his father Sydney in the Corporation Gas Department off the Birmingham Road in Stratford-upon-Avon, until like so many of his generation he followed his interest in flying and joined the RAF.

Arthur Aust.

In June 1944, the V-1 flying bomb offensive began. Of 6,725 that reached England, 2,420 fell on London. More than 6,000 people were killed and bomb damage was severe. The attacks played on people's nerves, and children were once again evacuated to the country. No. 68 Squadron took part in the campaign to intercept the flying bombs before they exploded on London and then turned their attention to those heavy bombers used to launch the V-1s over the North Sea, as well as continuing the patrols to counter enemy intruder aircraft over the east coast of England. During the last phase of the war the Allied strategic-bombing forces played a dominant part in bringing the German economy to the point of collapse.

On 4 March 1945, 234 aircraft (201 Halifax, twenty-one Lancaster and twelve Mosquito) attacked the synthetic-oil refinery at Bergkamen, north-east of Dortmund in North Rhine-Westphalia. That night in retaliation, the Luftwaffe quickly mounted Operation *Gisella*, sending 200 night fighters to follow the bombers to England. British defences were taken by surprise and the Germans shot down twenty bombers. Arthur Aust's Mosquito NT 357 'lost height on single-engine overshoot, his undercarriage failed to come down,' and at 3.44 am he crashed near his base at Coltishall.

Arthur's funeral was held in St James's Church in Guild Street in Stratford-upon-Avon. With the coffin draped in the Union flag, a squadron leader represented his commanding officer, fellow officers and aircrew of 68 Squadron, and there were friends from his time with the Corporation Gas Department and from school. He was buried in the cemetery on the Evesham Road, and his headstone reads:

One of the dearest
One of the best
He gave his life
That others might live!

Three days short of five years since Standish Mottram crashed in Suffolk to become the first Old Boy of King Edward VI to be killed in the Second World War, Arthur Aust, who was his contemporary at school, became the last. He is commemorated in the Garden of Remembrance in Old Town and in the Memorial Library at King Edward VI School.

Light me a candle in my memory
And let it burn for ever in your heart.
Flight Lieutenant Owen Chave, *Light Me a Candle*

Arthur's grave in Stratford Cemetery.

Notes
1. The county boundary changed in 1931, placing Preston-on-Stour in Warwickshire. The school closed in 1974.
2. The Stratford Bards XI continue to play their matches at Alscot Park.

Chapter 52

THEY HAVE PAID THE PRICE
OF FREEDOM

The names of those who in their lives fought for life,
Who wore at their hearts in fire's centre.
Born of the sun, they travelled a short while towards the sun,
And left the vivid air signed with their honour.
Stephen Spender

They were highly motivated brave young men and they had ideals. They fought for a cause in which they passionately believed. In them may be discerned the many faces of courage. Psychology writer Daniel Moran's principle asserts that courage is not an absolute human characteristic, but expendable capital every man possesses in varying quantity. In lonely cockpits, quartering the limitless sea, in unforgiving jungle, searching the hostile glare of the desert, and in the intensity of battle, their eyes were drawn towards horizons. As can only be understood by those who experience the possibility of death in war, they often stared toward infinity. Now they were there.

'They paid the price of freedom,' said their headmaster, the Reverend Cecil Knight, in a service at the Guild Chapel. 'It would be a price intolerable, unforgiveable, did we not know in our hearts that for them, and for all like them who gave their lives for England, the trumpets have sounded on the other side.' There was much talk of 'a new world' and 'after the war', but no talk of all the suffering, the anguish, the heartbreak. Many felt that life would never again be as sweet as before the war. As the evenings by the river Avon fused earth, sun and sky, these Old Boys of the school would live their unrealized lives in the memories of those they left behind.

Rejoice, whatever anguish rend your heart,
That God has given you for a priceless dower,
To live in these great times and have your part
in freedom's crowning hour;
That you may tell your sons who see the light
High in the heavens – their heritage to take –
'I saw the powers of darkness put to flight,
I saw the Morning break.'
Sir Owen Seaman

THE MEMORIAL LIBRARY

Wishing to commemorate those boys who had been lost in the First World War in a way that would be a lasting memorial to them, and would always be a tangible reminder to succeeding generations, the school governors agreed to the building of the Memorial Library in the south-west corner of the school quad. Composed of Warwickshire oak timber framing, the building was filled in between with plaster panels and with a brick lining, the whole being set on a plinth of local limestone. The interior was open to the roof, supported by two oak hammerbeam trusses, and the windows were filled in with lead lights, and some of the glass came from an old disused screen in Holy Trinity Church. The north window contained stained glass panels showing Henry V praying the night before the Battle of Agincourt, and was given by Mr and Mrs Howard Jennings in memory of their two sons. The bookcases and the bronze memorial tablet were

The dedication of the School Gates on Benefactors' Day. In the picture, left to right, are: Mr G.Q. Jaggard, the headmaster, Leslie Watkins, the Reverend E.F.S. Wilmot (reading from the service paper), the Reverend T.M. Parker and the Vicar (Canon Noel Prentice).

The Bishop of Coventry, Dr N.V. Gorton, dedicates the 1939-45 War Memorial in the Library.
Headmaster Leslie Watkins is on the left and Canon Noel Prentice on the right.

presented by the historian Sir George Trevelyan. The Library was formally opened
and blessed in May 1923. On Benefactors' Day in June 1955, an additional
memorial plaque with the names of those Old Boys killed in the Second World
War was dedicated. On the same day at the Church Street entrance to the school
by the Guildhall, the Old Boys' Association presented Memorial Gates dedicated
'to those who gave their lives in the 1939-1945 war'.

The Archive of the school is based in the Memorial Library.

IN GRATEFUL MEMORY OF
THE OLD BOYS OF KING EDWARDS SCHOOL
STRATFORD UPON AVON WHO LAID DOWN
THEIR LIVES IN THE SERVICE OF THEIR
COUNTRY IN THE GREAT WAR.
1914 - 1919

G. BALL	B. ELLIS
G.H.BARBER, M.C.	P. W. FISHER, D.C.M.
A. S. H.W. BARRETT	R. W. FISHER
J. A. BERRY	C. HOSKINS
A. G. BLOOMER	V. W. HYATT
W. J. BOARD	H. A. JENNINGS
H. CAVIS BROWN	H. H. JENNINGS
C. C. BRYAN, D.S.O.	J. D. LAMBERT
A. G. BURT	A. MORAY-BROWN
F. E. BURT	J. H. SAVAGE
F. BUTCHER	A. B. SMITH
F. BYRD	R. A. J. WARNEFORD, V.C.
R. C. CHAPPLE	A. WHATELEY
E. R. CLARKE	J. A. WILKES
G. B. DONALDSON	H. B. WILSON
	J. H. YELF

WHO DIES, IF ENGLAND LIVE?

1939 - 1945 WAR

A.J.AUST	R.HOLDER	C.H.ODELL	K.A.SMITH
F.J.BAILEY	T.W.JOY	J.P.ORGAN	R.W.O.SPENDER
S.C.BRIDGES-WILLIS	E.M.KENNARD	D.OVERBURY	J.G.STANLEY
G.F.CLARK	P.E.LOMAS	J.OVERBURY	D.TARVER
A.J.COGBILL	W.A.LOWTH	P.OVERTON	H.R.TAYLOR
C.J.COHU	R.H.MEGAINIY	T.S.R.PALMER	T.A.TESTAR
G.R.COLLINS	L.J.MERRITT	N.PARKES	R.F.TURNER
G.CROSS	J.G.MILLER	R.G.PARKS-SMITH	P.A.TYLER
P.ENGLISH	R.I.G.MILLER	S.R.PHILLIPS	M.P.WALTON
E.J.EVANS	J.P.MORRIS	F.C.PINFOLD	N.R.V.WATSON
L.HILLIER	S.C.MOTTRAM	F.G.ROTHERY	A.H.WOODWARD
P.S.A.HILLIER,D.F.C.	A.C.NORTH	H.SMITH	J.M.WYLEY
	W.J.STILES	T.C.HIATT	C.B.THORNTON

Memorial tablet.

ACKNOWLEDGEMENTS

For their kindness, enthusiasm and guidance I am very grateful to:

Derrick Smart, Peter Summerton, Steven Barker, Terry Harrison, John Testar, Bruce Tyler, Barbara McDonagh, Dorothy Houghton, Rosemary Sharman, Dr Douglas Bridgewater, Victor Church, Douglas Tuckey, Robert Higham, Patricia Joyce, Sally Miller, Carey and Chris Parkinson, Neville and Gwen Mellon, Bennet Carr, David Blake, Ron Hartill, Don Timms, Iain Panton, Gerry Tyack MBE, Maretta Pearson, Sue Hirons, Gordon Stokes, Julie Salt, Michael Hawley, Keith Perry, Michael Wells, Pip Stowell, Brian Howett, John Larder, Christopher Badbury, E.A. Norman, Peter Kazmierczak, Hans Houterman, The Royal Hampshire Regiment Trust, The Commonwealth War Graves Commission at Leamington Spa, Henry Wilson, Matt Jones, Linne Matthews and Sylvia Menzies-Earl.

Grateful thanks and acknowledgement for the use of photographs to Brian Adams, Mohamed Arebi, The Arnold Scheme, Steven Barker, Michael Caldwell, Bruce Tyler, John Testar, Jersey Heritage, Patricia Joyce, RAF Fiskerton, Julie Salt and Brian Watson.

The pictures and photographs in this book have been obtained from many different sources, and some are second- or third-hand copies, which explains their quality.

FURTHER READING

The following magazines and books were consulted for reference and inspiration, and all are gratefully acknowledged:

Magazines
Aircraft magazine: March 2011
TIME magazine: 28 April 1941; 23 June 1941

Books
Ambrose, Stephen E.: *Wild Blue* (Simon & Schuster, 2001)
Baker, Paul: *Yeoman Yeoman – The Warwickshire Yeomanry 1920-1956* (The Queen's Own Warwickshire and Worcestershire Yeomanry Regimental Association, 1971)
Barker, Ralph: *The Thousand Plan* (Airlife Publishing, 1992)
Bayly, Christopher and Harper, Tim: *Forgotten Armies* (Penguin, 2004)
Beaton, Cecil: *Winged Squadrons* (Hutchinson, 1942)
Bierman, John and Smith, Colin: *Alamein – War Without Hate* (Penguin Viking, 2002)
Bishop, Patrick: *Battle of Britain* (Quercus, 2010)
Bishop, Patrick: *Bomber Boys* (Harper Perennial, 2008)
Bishop, Patrick: *Fighter Boys* (Harper Perennial, 2008)
Botting, Douglas: *The D-Day Invasion* (Time-Life Books, 1978)
Ciardi, John: *Selected Poems* (University of Arkansas Press, 1984)
Collins, William: *A Short History of the Stratford-upon-Avon Boat Club* (George Boydon and Son, 1974)
Crook, David: *Spitfire Pilot* (Greenhill Books, 2006)
Doherty, Richard: *A Noble Crusade* (Spellmount, 1999)
Doherty, Richard: *The British Reconnaissance Corps in World War II* (Osprey, 2007)
Fallada, Hans: *Alone in Berlin* (Penguin Classics, 1994)
Faulks, Sebastian: *The Fatal Englishman* (Vintage, 1997)
Fogg, Nicholas: *Stratford: A Town at War 1914-1945* (Sutton Publishing, 2008)
Ford, Ken: *Dieppe 1942* (Osprey Publishing 2003)
Gellhorn, Martha: *The Face of War* (Granta Books, 1998)
Goss, Chris: *Brothers in Arms* (Crecy Publishing, 1994)
Hastings, Max: *All Hell Let Loose* (Harper Press, 2011)
Hastings, Max: *Armageddon* (Macmillan, 2004)
Hastings, Max: *Bomber Command* (Pan Books, 1999)

FURTHER READING

Homes, Richard: *The Oxford Companion to Military History* (OUP, 2001)
Jarrell, Randall: *Collected Poems* (Farrar, Straus and Giroux, 1969)
Keegan, John: *The Second World War* (Viking Press, 1990)
Kershaw, Ian: *Hitler – Nemesis* (Allen Lane, 2000)
Largent, Willard: *RAF Wings Over Florida: Memories of World War II British Air Cadets* (Purdue University Press, 2000)
Latimer, Jon: *Burma: The Forgotten War* (John Murray, 2004)
Lavey, Brian: *Churchill's Navy* (Conway, 2006)
MacDonald, Callum: *The Killing of SS Obergruppenführer Reinhard Heydrich* (Macmillan, 1989)
Majdalany, Fred: *Cassino* (Longmans, 1959)
Milner, Marc: *Battle of the Atlantic* (Tempus Publishing, 2003)
Monsarrat, Nicholas: *The Cruel Sea* (Cassell and Co, 1951)
Munson, K.: *Aircraft of World War II* (Ian Allan, 1962)
Orr, David and Truesdale, David: *The Rifles are There* (Pen & Sword, 2005)
Parsons, Rev. Laurie: *A History of Radford Semele* (Radford Semele PCC, 1974)
Ramsey, Winston G.: *The Battle of Britain Then and Now* (After the Battle, 1982)
Rhodes, Peter: *For a Shilling a Day* (Bank House Books, 2010)
Richards, Jeffrey: *Happiest Days* (MUP, 1991)
Richie, Alexandra: *Faust's Metropolis* (Harper Collins, 1999)
Saunders, Hilary St George: *Royal Air Force 1939-1945, Volumes I to III* (Her Majesty's Stationery Office, 1954)
Smith, Colin: *England's Last War Against France* (Orion Books, 2010)
Swift, Daniel: *Bomber County* (Hamish Hamilton, 2010)
The Battle of Britain (His Majesty's Stationery Office, 1941)
Thompson, R.W.: *Dieppe at Dawn* (Arrow, 1958)
Waller, Jane and Vaughan-Rees, Michael: *Blitz – The Civilian War* (Optima, 1990)
Woolf, Virginia: *The Diary of* (Hogarth Press, 1977)
Wynn, Kenneth W.: *Men of the Battle of Britain* (CCB Associates, 1999)

INDEX

Tracing Your Family History?

Read Your Family HISTORY

ESSENTIAL ADVICE FROM THE EXPERTS

FREE COPY!

Your Family History is the only magazine that is put together by expert genealogists. Our editorial team, led by Dr Nick Barratt, is passionate about family history, and our networks of specialists are here to give essential advice, helping readers to find their ancestors and solve those difficult questions.

In each issue we feature a **Beginner's Guide** covering the basics for those just getting started, a **How To** … section to help you to dig deeper into your family tree and the opportunity to **Ask The Experts** about your tricky research problems. We also include a **Spotlight** on a different county each month and a **What's On** guide to the best family history courses and events, plus much more.

Receive a free copy of *Your Family History* magazine and gain essential advice and all the latest news. To request a free copy of a recent back issue, simply e-mail your name and address to marketing@your-familyhistory.com or call 01226 734302*.

Your Family History is in all good newsagents and also available on subscription for six or twelve issues. For more details on how to take out a subscription, call 01778 392013 or visit **www.your-familyhistory.co.uk**.

Alternatively read issue 31 online completely free using this QR code

www.your-familyhistory.com